D1407984

TAMING MONSTERS, SLAYING DRAGONS

TAMING MONSTERS, SLAYING DRAGONS

*The Revolutionary Family Approach to
Overcoming Childhood Fears and Anxiety*

by Joel Feiner, M.D. *AND GRAHAM YOST*

ARBOR HOUSE   *William Morrow • New York*

Copyright © 1988 by G. S. Sharpe Communications, Inc.

All rights reserved. No part of this book may be reproduced or utilized in any form or by any means, electronic or mechanical, including photocopying, recording, or by any information storage and retrieval system, without permission in writing from the Publisher. Inquiries should be addressed to Permissions Department, Arbor House, William Morrow and Company, Inc., 105 Madison Avenue, New York, N.Y. 10016.

Manufactured in the United States of America

Published in Canada by Fitzhenry & Whiteside Ltd.

10 9 8 7 6 5 4 3 2 1

Library of Congress Cataloging-in-Publication Data

Feiner, Joel.
    Taming monsters, slaying dragons: the revolutionary family approach to overcoming childhood fears and anxiety / by Joel Feiner and Graham Yost.
        p.   cm.
    Bibliography: p.
    Includes index.
    ISBN: 0-87795-939-0
    1. Fear in children. 2. Phobias in children. 3. Anxiety in children. 4. Family psychotherapy. I. Yost, Graham. II. Title.
RJ506.P38F45   1988
618.92′8522—dc19   87-23750
                              CIP

Excerpt from *World's Fair* by E.L. Doctorow, copyright © 1985. A Fawcett Crest Book, published by Ballantine Books by arrangement with Random House, Inc.

"The Fears of Childhood," modified and reproduced from *Treating Children's Fears and Phobias: A Behavioral Approach* by R. Morris and T. Kratochwill, copyright © 1983 by Pergamon Press. Used with permission.

"The Social Readjustment Scale," adapted from T.H. Holmes and R.H. Rahe, *Journal of Psychosomatic Research,* Vol. 11, 1967, 213–18, copyright © by Pergamon Press. Used with permission.

To Helen and Sol Feiner, the parents in my house,
and to all other parents everywhere.

—JOEL FEINER, M.D.

To Mary Illingworth and Crystal Greene,
two friends who helped this particular child
with his fears and anxiety.

—GRAHAM YOST

In seconds I am washed, powdered, clean-clothed, and brought to secret smiles in the dark. I ride, the young prince, in her arms to their bed, and am welcomed between them, in the blessed dry warmth between them. My father gives me a companionable pat and falls back to sleep with his hand on my shoulder. Soon, they are both asleep. I smell their godlike odors, male, female. A moment later, as the faintest intimation of daylight appears as an outline of the window shade, I am wide awake, blissful, guarding my sleeping parents, the terrible night past me, the dear day about to dawn.

—E. L. Doctorow
World's Fair

Contents

Acknowledgments

Networks and support systems have become unfortunate jargon. The concepts and especially the reality, though, are rich and sustaining. The network got this book underway and sustained the effort. Genell Subak-Sharpe is the hub, with the connection instigated by Mel Roman, leading then to our agent, Barbara Lowenstein, and the co-conspirator, Graham Yost. Thanks to them all.

The support system is the necessary nutrient in my life, and I have learned what it means by living it. Love, fun, competence, reciprocity, loyalty, trust, security—all those things that ward off the ultimate fear and make this enterprise worthwhile. The starting team is Ron, Donna, Daniel, and Anna—we have been tested and we have come through. The cousins . . . without whom . . . The friends who know who they are. Teachers, students, trainees, colleagues, patients—those of you who make up the absorbing, living, vital, creative, professional dimension of my life—and the individuals who defy these categories, but whose resources and assistance were vital in this undertaking— Jane Weiss, Carol Pastures, Maureen Kaylor, Kathy Sharon and Fred Krassner. And finally, my heartfelt appreciation to the parents and children who have spoken with me so openly, willingly, and well.

TAMING
MONSTERS,
SLAYING
DRAGONS

Introduction

All of us can look back on our childhood and recall objects or situations that filled us with fear. One of my most vivid childhood memories involves trying to convince my brother who was then about three years old, that it was safe for him to leave our house. He had accidentally stepped on a baby bird, and was terrified that the mother bird was lurking outside, waiting to punish him for killing her baby. My own fear of the dark, when I was about the same age, lingered for several years and was a source of disagreement between my brother and myself. I couldn't go to sleep in the room we shared unless the light was on, and he insisted that the light kept him awake. Our parents finally worked out a compromise—they left the hall light on and our door open just a crack.

When I was about seven or eight, I was struggling with the meaning of death. I remember lying in my bed at night, working out how many more years my parents, grandparents, uncles, aunts, and other relatives had to live (while at the same time practicing arithmetic). To those I was particularly fond of I assigned a lifespan of a hundred years. But even so, I was terrified by the receding numbers, and fearful that they would be carried off before I was ready for them to go. Couldn't I find a way to control the process?

With the benefit of hindsight and years of practicing family therapy, I can now look back on these personal experiences with deeper understanding and nagging questions. Why was I the one my family deputized to deal with my brother's fears? (And why do I still assume this role for so many others, even though we are middle-aged adults?) And what influence did this early familial experience have on my selecting medicine, or more specifically psychiatry and family therapy, as a career? Was I so taken with the role of helping my brother that I chose to devote my career to extending this to others?

Daily, I encounter patients who are seeking help in dealing with their own fears and anxieties. I am constantly reminded that children in particular live in a fear-filled world that we adults often have a hard time remembering or envisioning. The lion in the vacuum cleaner, the monsters that live under the bed or in the closet, the wicked witches that come out at night to eat little boys and girls are but a few common, and very normal, childhood fears, which almost always disappear on their own. Other fears are rooted in disasters (the hurricane that destroys the family home, the serious illness or death of a parent or grandparent) or major disruptions in the family (the arrival of a new baby or divorce of the parents). Still others by major concerns of our time—nuclear war, AIDS, the Challenger disaster. Most common, however, are fears propagated by what is going on in the family at the time. They persist on behalf of the family, helping to protect the family from the possibility of something worse happening. Helping parents to understand and deal with these fears and anxieties is the purpose of this book.

How we respond to a child's fears and anxieties in large part determines whether they will become problems. Not long ago I had a call from a former college classmate who was very concerned over his five-year-old son's fear of his parents going out in the evening. Tim did not seem to have problems when his father went off to work in the morning or when his mother left him with a sitter during the day. But he would cry for hours if they attempted to leave him with a sitter in the evening. "I just can't deal with his carrying on," the father told me, barely hiding his anger. "I swear he resents our going off for a few hours to be by ourselves."

Maybe, I thought, but I suspected that other factors were at work here. Discussions with the parents and Tim revealed several that were relevant. Tim's behavior inevitably resulted in an argument between his parents, and on a couple of occasions, his mother had been reduced to tears and ended up staying home. At first the parents tried to reason with Tim. "We are leaving you in charge," his mother said. "Sally will be here if you need her." To Tim, being in charge meant that he suddenly was responsible for himself, his baby sister, the house, dog, everything; an understandably frightening prospect for a five-year-old. The fact that he could call on Sally for help was of little comfort. Gentle probing revealed that what also worried Tim was the conviction that his parents would die in a car accident, and he would be left to take care of the baby all by himself. An incident like this had happened on a television program, and had made a big impression on Tim as did violent crashes on TV News. He did not understand that the sibling in the TV story was much older, and that it was all make-believe anyway. Tim could not begin to imagine how he would be able to take over for his parents, so the best alternative was to keep them safely at home. When he tried this, it provoked an argument between his parents, and at least part of the time his mother sided with Tim and stayed home. Further probing found that the parents had been arguing a good deal lately, mostly about the mother's wish to resume her career. My friend, although sympathetic to his wife's career ambitions, came from a close-knit, traditional family where the mother stayed home with the children and the father was the breadwinner. Deep down, he looked upon his wife's return to the work-place as an indication that he was an inadequate provider. Mother had same unacknowledged mixed feelings, such as, could she do it all and played out one part of the ambivalence by acting in alliance with her son. Granted, they were having some financial problems, but nothing he couldn't work out. With all this going on, it was little wonder that Tim was becoming fearful and anxious whenever his parents began making plans to go out for the evening.

After Tim's parents understood the basis of Tim's fears and how their own "spouse" issues exacerbated the problem, they were able to deal with the situation in an effective manner. Instead of leaving Tim in charge, they, as one voice, assured him: "There is very little chance that anything is going to happen to us, but just in case something does, you have Grandma and Grandpa and Uncle Bill, who will take care of you and Amy. And Sally is here to take care of both of you and everything else until we come back. We know you will be safe while we are gone, and we'll be safe too." What was critical, however, was that the parents were now acting in concert. They no longer undermined each other; they were an effective coali-tion.

Tim also could understand and accept the explanation from both parents and was further reassured by their safe re-turn. It did not take too long for the separation anxiety to abate. Not all childhood fears are this obvious or easy to solve, but this case underscores the central theme of this book.

Above all, this is a book for and about families. Every family follows a developmental path, with inevitable disrup-tions and crises. In facing any change or crisis, a family needs to draw on its resources. In times of conflict or trouble, children are inevitably drawn into the parental dyad. Children are also the most vulnerable members of the family system and, as such, often become the focus of a family's heightened reaction to a crisis. This can lead to feelings of anxiety and fear. Regardless of what caused the problem originally, the child's fear now becomes a necessary part of the family's need to maintain its equilibrium. But wouldn't it be better if the family group didn't have to expend so much energy fighting the demons within? Operating as a well functioning group they can face the complex outside world together and connect with others to become part of a *community*.

In the pages that follow, we will take you through the structure of a family system and show how the system operates in everyday life. You will learn how to tell effective coping techniques from those that are detrimental, and why it is so vital that families work together in dealing with problems confronting one of its members. Although a child's fear may be the most obvious symptom, the cure is not likely to be found in treating the child, but instead in treating the entire family or system.

You will find that most of the time you will be able to analyze and solve the problem without outside help. But you will learn how to recognize those instances in which professional help is indicated and where you should go to get it. The family-system concepts we emphasize in this book may be new to you, but in the end we think you will agree that they are so logical and obvious that it is a wonder they are only now gaining a following.

Throughout this book, we cite cases that are drawn from my own practice or that of close associates. We have disguised the names, but the situations described are real. In searching back through these cases and examining my own experiences as a family therapist and medical educator, I have become even more convinced of the validity of dealing with childhood fears and anxieties in their larger context—the family unit.

An important note: in this book, we will use the two-parent model for the family for two reasons. First, though in this country the number of two-parent families has been in steady decline as the number of single-parent families has been on the rise, the two-parent family is still the most prevalent. Second, and more important, every family, whether there are actually two parents together and married at the head of the family, has two people in authority roles, especially during stressful times.

There does not even have to be a person there to fill the role. Indeed, a parent who died or abandoned the family is still likely to continue to influence the family, if only as an idea (that is often much of the family's problem—the effect that this shadow parent can still have). In other cases, the other "parent" may be a grandparent, an older child, a social worker, a good friend, a teacher; for, as we will see in a later chapter, human relationships always work in threes, even when a third person does not seem so apparent.

So, throughout this book, when we speak of "parents," what we say can be applied to the experience of the single parent and his or her co-parent, whether or not he or she is married to that person or whether or not that person is around or even alive. The way things work as a family will be similar (although the single parent's job is undeniably harder).

1 Children's Fears in Historic Perspective

Rob and Laura were excited about getting their young son, Richie, a pet. When Rob brought home a big dog he was sure Richie would jump for joy. Imagine his surprise when, instead, Richie ran away in mortal terror and hid in a kitchen cabinet until the dog was taken away.

If you watched TV in the early 1960s, you might recognize the above "case history" as an episode of "The Dick Van Dyke Show." Richie was terrified of the dog, convinced that it would eat him whole, until his parents allayed his fear (not, of course, without some comic mistakes along the way) by showing him that the dog was gentle and more afraid of Richie than Richie was of it. Happy conclusion of the episode's dilemma, a humorous coda, bring up theme, roll credits, into a commercial and on to the next show.

Of course, as all parents know, life does not work quite so smoothly. It does not come in convenient, self-contained thirty- or sixty-minute segments. Certainly some families find that, on occasion, they are close to the TV family model, and their children are coached out of their fears without too much trouble in a relatively short period of time. But other families find that their Richie's fear of dogs does not vanish so quickly. It might last weeks, months, or years, perhaps even disabling the boy and disrupting the life of the family.

A fear can assume grand proportions. A seven-year-old girl

with severe school phobia may find her education threatened. A boy who panics during electrical storms may have the awful discomfort of hyperventilation added to his fear. And the effect of the fear can go beyond the child. A child's fear of deep water can color a family's summer vacation at the lake. A child's fear of going to sleep can turn parents into sleepless walking zombies within a matter of days.

This book is about problematic childhood fears. Although we will cover the nature of all childhood fears and how they develop, our primary concern is with those fears that become a serious problem, both for the child and for the whole family— the ones that linger, that do not go away, and particularly those that seem to occupy all of the family's energies.

We take what most readers will find to be a new approach to problem childhood fears. We focus on the family—how a child's fear affects the family, how the family's response to the fear can either help it vanish or sustain it, and how the fear begins to exist, not within a child's mind, but within the life of the family.

How is this different or new? In the past, most approaches to childhood fears have focused on the child—what is wrong with him or her and how do you treat the child? The assumption has been that if only "naive," "unsophisticated," but well-meaning parents could understand children the way professionals do, the fears would go away.

We believe that although certain fears are a natural part of childhood, fears that evolve into problems are less common, and usually they only become problems when the family responds to them in a way that doesn't allow them to disappear by themselves. The reality, as we all know, is not that parents simply do not have the "right knowledge" to deal with the fear, but that the family's life is very complex, and the child's fear may fit into this complexity. It may sound at first that this approach attacks and blames families. We hope to show that just the opposite is true—it is the family that has the power to help and heal its members. This family-oriented approach is new; childhood fears have not been dealt with this way traditionally.

Sigmund Freud and Little Hans

Freud's case history of Little Hans was the first and most famous case history of a child with a worrisome fear. Little Hans's problem was a pathological horse phobia. A sensitive youth, he had seen one beaten in a merry-go-round, and later a horse pulling a carriage he was in fell. From then on, all things equine terrified him.

Freud's analysis of the case was that Little Hans had transferred his Oedipal fear of his father onto horses. The basic idea of the Oedipal phase is that, somewhat like the Greek tragic character Oedipus, who killed his father and (inadvertently) slept with his mother, males have a deep desire to maintain and increase an intensely held bond with their mothers and therefore bear malice toward fathers, who stand in the way and are feared because they can seem like big and strong and severe rivals (the development of females during this period is still controversial in psychoanalytic theory). Young males are uncomfortable with these fears and fantasies of aggression—which, in fact, seem downright dangerous—and so they may sometimes unconsciously transfer them, superimposing them on something or someone else. According to Freud, Little Hans imbued horses with all the fear and apprehension he really felt about his father.

To be highly simplistic, Freud's overall view of fears was that they are a combination of the anxiety created by the internal struggle in our "unconscious" to control our desires (such as what Little Hans went through) and symbolic fears (a fear of snakes may be related to concerns about genitals). His method of treatment was psychoanalysis—helping the patient to understand the underlying causes in past history or past mental life persisting in the unconscious, and by gaining that insight, gain mastery over the present problem. What may have been appropriate and helpful in the past is currently "extra baggage" and no longer necessary for survival. Psychoanalysis helps to develop and enforce that conviction. In the case of Little Hans, Freud dealt with the boy's father, and when the boy's father was able to understand the Oedipal nature of Hans's fear of horses, he was then able to help his son through the fear, allowing him to express his fear and anger more directly and learn that the fearful hidden fantasy had no basis in reality.

The Behavioralists and Little Albert

Some researchers and theorists in the 1920s did not agree with Freud's approach to fears. Although admitting that a fear of snakes could have something to do with a fear of one's father, or something to do with penis envy or castration anxiety, to them that was not the point. The unconscious was a Freudian construct that did not interest them, in part because it could not be subjected to experimental validation. They believed fears were learned through experience. Much as Pavlov's dogs "learned" to salivate when they heard the ring of a bell they had come to associate with mealtime, so these researchers theorized that we "learn" fears when we associate a particular object or situation with a feeling of fear; for example, having had a bad experience while getting a tooth filled, Bill becomes pathologically afraid of going to the dentist.

To these theorists, then, fear is a *conditioned response.* To prove this, two researchers in the 1920s conditioned an infant, dubbed Little Albert, to fear fluffy white things by making a frighteningly loud noise every time he reached for a fluffy white thing. It worked. Although they never got a chance to test it out (Albert's mother removed him from the experiment), they also believed fear could be "unlearned" or counterconditioned.

Counterconditioning is now the most widely used form of treatment for problem fears and phobias. By becoming slowly and systematically desensitized (like treating an allergy by gradually subjecting a person to increasing amounts of the allergenic substance), by learning to relax because the experience of relaxation is incompatible with anxiety, by watching someone else master the feared object or situation, or by changing thoughts associated with the fear (cognitive restructuring) people's fear behavior can be modified—hence the name for the treatment, *behavior modification therapy.*

Newton's Legacy

Despite the fact that the Freudian psychodynamic view of fears and the behavioralist position are somewhat opposed, they do have something in common—they are both predicated on the concept of linear cause and effect. Underlying both Freud and the behavioralists is the idea that the human mind is like a machine, and that if you know everything that has gone into the machine, you will be able to figure out why the machine is behaving in a certain way and, better still, will be able to predict what will happen in the future (that is, by controlling or knowing the input you can control the output).

According to this view, life is a series of events, each one causing the succeeding one. It is as though everything is being played out on a pool table. Theoretically, knowing the mechanics of cause and effect, you could, after the last ball is sunk in the pocket, retrace the entire game, following back through all the collisions and combinations of collisions to discover how the first ball was shot.

This view is a legacy of Newtonian physics. Newton's achievements in mathematics and physics were astounding, and with them he forged a rigorous way of looking at the world, a way of finding out how things worked. This "scientific method" seemed capable of explaining everything. Indeed, by the end of the nineteenth century, the feeling was that science was just about over, that except for a few details and data, every mystery had been explained. Of course, as all mystery readers know, as soon as someone boldly declares that the mystery has been solved a few new clues are always found that do not quite fit the solution.

An underlying precept of Newtonian physics is that everything exists in degrees on a continuum—there are no radical jumps in nature, just different points on a smooth progression. If you heat a piece of iron, it should glow red when heated moderately, then slowly progress through the spectrum until, if hot enough, it emits blue-white light. Experiments, however, showed that the progression is not so smooth, and that, contrary to what Newton had led scientists to expect, there is a sudden and abrupt jump from red to blue.

In 1900, Max Planck, a confirmed Newtonian, discovered, much to his chagrin, that the electrons responsible for emitting energy do not work as degrees on a continuum, but come in discrete packets, which he dubbed *quanta.* A few years later, Albert Einstein discovered that light, which had been thought to be wavelike, also came in discrete packets, which he called *photons.*

Later, Einstein challenged another basic Newtonian principle. According to Newtonian physics, if you stand at the front of a moving train and throw a ball forward, the velocity of the ball, relative to the ground, will equal the velocity of the train plus the velocity given the ball by throwing it. Logically, this should also apply to shining a flashlight off the front of the train—the light's velocity should be the speed of light, plus that of the train. Einstein found that this is not the case. He discovered that the speed of light, in a vacuum, is constant, regardless of its context—it is always 186,000 miles per second, never more or less. This discovery came under his landmark "Special Theory of Relativity."

Planck's quantum physics and Einstein's relativity are not theories we use in our day-to-day lives (indeed, very few of us can even understand them). They operate on the extremes of existence—the very, very tiny and the very, very large and fast. You drive to work in a car that operates on Newtonian principles, not on the theory of relativity. Nevertheless, these thoughts did change the way the universe was viewed. Newton's ideas were once thought to represent absolute truth. But with the discoveries of Planck and Einstein, Newton's view was found to be simply one way of looking at things. The Newtonian universe was revealed to be not the universe itself, but a model of the universe—a *paradigm*. Einstein, Planck, and the many particle, quantum, and astrophysicists who have succeeded them were responsible for radically changing the paradigm.

The New Paradigm

Now, you might wonder, what does quantum physics have to do with childhood fears? Well, just as the paradigm (model) for the view of the physical universe has changed, so has the paradigm for the view of the mind, and along similar paths. It seems that the consequence of a new scientific model is its use in forging a new model of the mind.

As we saw, despite their differences, psychoanalysts and behavioralists both see the mind as something of a black box—if you could study all the input, you could predict the output through the principle of cause and effect. And if you could *control* the input, you could get the output you desired: the mind as machine.

But about the middle of this century, some people began to question the idea of linear cause and effect. They noticed that on many occasions causality is *circular.* It is not a chain of events (A causes B, which causes C, which causes D, and so on), but rather a loop or circle that continually recauses itself (A causes B, which causes C, which causes A again, which causes B, and so on).

This circular causality implies that *what happened in the past is not always important.* The decision on exactly what the root cause is may have to be a rather arbitrary one. Did A start it all by causing B, or did C start it all by causing A? Might there not be something that came before A, B, or C?

You may recognize this as the old "chicken-or-egg" puzzle. But these theorists, instead of debating which came first, discarded the question. Their position was that if you cannot determine which came first, the chicken or the egg, then maybe it doesn't matter. Maybe all that does matter is that there are chickens and eggs and that the cycle continues.

In other words, whatever event it was that started the circular causality is not as important as how that circular loop keeps on perpetuating itself. We can stop asking *why*, which deals with ultimate beginnings (which may only exist when we arbitrarily fix a starting point for the process), and start asking *how* and *what*.

How does this apply to psychology? Well, imagine a wife who is recovering from a suicide attempt. She says she did it because her husband had an affair. He counters that he only had the affair because she was so distant. She says she was only distant because he never paid attention to her. He says . . . It could go on and on, with no "cause" in sight. Indeed, even if one could be found, would it matter? The problem is that husband and wife have entered a loop of circular causality—both their actions and reactions have become mutually supporting—not that one of them "did something" to the other. In this loop of interactions, each response modifies the other person's response to the response.

Suppose the wife went into therapy by herself. Would that solve the problem? If the problem is how the two of them are interacting, wouldn't it be better for them both to work on the *pattern* of their interaction together, rather than just focus on the behavior of only one of the participants? Individual therapy might change her and, therefore, the loop to a degree, but would a resolution to the interaction problem necessarily be guaranteed?

This goes against the view of traditional psychology, which is to treat the individual. The new idea is to treat, not the individual, but the *context*. The family is usually the most important context in our lives, and it operates as a group, as a unit, differently than a random collection of individuals. The family members' life together, their interactions and relationships, are patterned. Symptoms can then be seen, not as manifestations of problems within the individual, but as manifestations of problems within the context; not *within* people, but *among* people.

And so, this "new psychology" is founded on the belief that what happens with the individual is substantially a function of what is going on in the family. The new approach is to discern the patterns in the family and, if dysfunctional, to work to shake the patterns from their rigidity. It has also been called an "ecological" model because it emphasizes *"connectedness."*

In the traditional paradigm of mind as machine, treating the problem was a matter of figuring out what was wrong with the *individual* and then working on that. In the new paradigm of the family, treating the problem involves treating the family. This approach is known as *family therapy*.

How does this apply to childhood fears? Virtually all children experience fears at one point or another; but most of them go away. Trouble comes when those fears do not go away, and the reason they remain is often rooted in how the family reacted to the fear. What is important is not so much how the fear was caused (being scared by a big dog, seeing *Jaws* on TV, copying a parent's fear of heights), which may long since be forgotten, but how the family—usually one with subtle or overt difficulties—has reacted to it in a way that sustains it. If that sustaining response can be changed, the fear will most likely no longer serve a function for the family and can then be treated directly or allowed to simply disappear, as most fears usually do.

This, then, is the basic premise of this book—all children have fears, but a fear usually becomes serious only when there is something in the way the child's family responds to the fear that sustains or perhaps even exaggerates it. The fear begins to be incorporated into the family's way of functioning and is needed as a distraction so that something even worse may be avoided. Perhaps the fear can be resolved by treating the child alone, but likely other family issues, more troublesome, may remain. Ultimately this means that the best way to treat a problem childhood fear is to look at the whole family, not just the child.

Where We Are Going

We will attempt to cover all aspects of childhood fears—where they come from, how they are sustained, and what contributes to their being sustained. In order to do this, we will have to introduce some of the special ways of thinking about how a family functions as a unit. We will look at the family as a system and see how it works as one. We will see what traits and characteristics are associated with the healthy family system and how structures within the family, specifically *triangles, boundaries,* and *subsystems,* determine how the family system functions. We will see how the basic ground rules of good communication can help prevent a family from sustaining a child's fears.

We will discuss the common, normal fears of childhood and how the nature of these fears is determined by the child's stage of development. We also will look at the various kinds of stress, for a family's state of health and its ability to cope with and dispel childhood fears is most apparent when the family is under stress. We will see how important support systems are in modifying the effects of stress.

Finally, we will look at the specifics of how families can deal with childhood fears, how families can help themselves, using their own resources, or by availing themselves of family therapy, the clinical application of the ideas we are discussing.

Looking at the problems of the individual in terms of his or her context may seem to some a very new, somewhat radical idea. Indeed, this approach has only been around for about forty years—not very long in the scheme of things. But that's long enough to demonstrate one very important fact about this new paradigm—it works.

2 Family Systems

In the 1930s, researchers who studied various biological interactions began to notice that everything works in systems. They discovered that human relationships are systems, and that they work much along the lines of the mechanized systems that we have created in industry. Like computer circuitry, human systems can, to a large degree, be "flow-charted." An example of this is an organized workplace, where the structure, various roles, levels of authority and responsibility, and channels of communication can be clearly diagrammed. Other human systems are schools and groups of friends. But the primary human system is the family.

Along with this systems study came the idea of circular causality. The two fit together well.

Some psychologists began to wonder if the root "causes" of a problem (if one could be found) mattered far less than *how* the problem was propagated and sustained in the system by enduring patterns. By viewing a patient's symptoms in context—in terms of the individual's relationship with his or her family and the family's patterns and how the patient functioned consistently within that system—they began to see that these symptoms can often be used by the family system to achieve stability or status quo in the face of some other disruptive stress.

These family systems pioneers discovered a model for the way families use such potentially harmful symptoms to maintain the status quo. They noticed how some machines are built with self-regulating devices, such as engines that shut off when they get too hot. These researchers began to think of the family as just such a self-correcting system. They found that most of the time this self-regulation is fine—families need to correct and adjust and adapt. Problems arise, however, when that which the family uses to stabilize itself, to keep itself on course, is a psychological problem, a response that is unhealthy and eventually harmful.

A classic example is common childhood school phobia:

For weeks Suzy Roberts has been gearing up for school, but now, on the day she is to go, she suddenly gets scared. She doesn't want to go. Janey, her mother, gets angry, but finally gives in and lets Suzy stay home. But this isn't a one-time occurrence. It gets so that almost every weekday morning Suzy will complain of an upset stomach or some other ailment. Janey suspects it's a ploy, tries to force her daughter to go, but doesn't get anywhere and ends up giving in. Janey's husband, Pete, very busy at work, only gets involved to the extent of telling his wife that it's her responsibility to see that Suzy goes to school.

The symptoms might make it look like Suzy is simply pathologically afraid of going to school, when, in fact, she is really afraid of leaving home, because she senses her mother does not want her to leave. Why?

Perhaps it is as simple as Janey not wanting to be left alone during the day. It's unlikely, however, that that fear of being alone would be so disruptive unless it too represented something else. Maybe Janey needs Suzy's company because she already feels distanced from Pete, who spends so much time at work. It would then seem that Pete is the "cause" of the problem. Not so, he might reply; he spends so much time at work not only because he has to "put bread on the table," but also because he feels excluded from a too close relationship that has emerged at home between his wife and daughter.

Another example:

> *Marty is having awful trouble with stomach cramps. His parents, Audrey and Les, seem to think it has something to do with his digestion (the cramps often come after dinner), but they aren't sure. They do notice though that the cramps subside when they give him attention, which leads Les to think that maybe the cramps are just a way for Marty to get attention. Audrey thinks that's a terrible thing to accuse their son of. Les insists he's right. They begin to fight. Before they know it Marty is complaining of cramps again.*

Les is right—to an extent. His son *is* trying to gain attention, but not because he craves the spotlight. He gets stomach pains every time his parents start to fight, for by drawing attention to himself (probably not a conscious decision) he distracts them from their problems as spouses and unites them as parents. And the parents support this arrangement, preferring it to an escalating battle.

In the cases of both Suzy's school phobia and Marty's stomach cramps, what is most useful in correcting the situation is not determining what "caused" the symptoms, but what sustains them and allows them to persist—the need for the family to stabilize a problem elsewhere in the system. There is no one cause; rather, the causality is circular, the pattern of the triangle ritualized, and the symptoms of the individual (Marty's stomach pains, Suzy's school phobia) become the symptoms of the whole family system. The blame is not individual oriented but *systemic.*

The complexity of the system's response is evident in the following case history:

> *Dave Sawchuk is a bright, active five-year-old boy with a common fear for a five-year-old: monsters. For a while it was under control. All it took was for either his mother, Lisa, or father, Mark, to check Dave's bedroom for monsters (with appropriate calling under the bed and sudden opening of the closet door to surprise any lurking goblin) to allow Dave to rest easy. But it hasn't been getting better; in fact, it's been getting worse. Dave is now so terrified of monsters in his room that he can't sleep there and has been spending most nights in his parents' bed. No matter how carefully and forcefully they explain that there are no such things as monsters, Mark and Lisa find Dave's fear unflagging.*

The traditional approach to Dave's fear might be a course of *systematic desensitization*—his parents or a therapist would slowly make him feel more comfortable in his room and would give him a sense of mastery over his fear of monsters. That course of action might work. But it ignores the possibility that Dave's fear is playing a role, serving a function in the family. To find out if that is the case, one would have to find out what else is going on in the Sawchuk family.

> *The biggest change in their life is indeed a major one— they moved across the country. Since before Dave was born, Mark and Lisa had been living in Manhattan. Six months ago, however, Lisa, a public relations executive, got an offer with a large firm in Los Angeles. They knew Mark,*

*an entertainment agent, would be able to find work in L.A.,
so they decided to move. Used to the relatively confined
atmosphere of a New York apartment, they were delighted
to have their very own house in Sherman Oaks. But with
every new situation comes new concerns. Lisa had grown
accustomed to the threat of crime in New York, but crime
in L.A. was new. In New York there seemed to be unwritten
rules—she knew what streets were safe and what ones
weren't, when she could ride the subway and when she
couldn't. But she didn't know those rules in L.A., or even
if there were any. From what she read in the papers, crime
in L.A. seemed more random, as if there was less one could
do about it. When she drove home one day and saw police
cars and an ambulance on a neighboring street, her fear
began to mount.*

It doesn't take a great leap to see how Lisa's growing fear
of crime and criminals could be learned by her son and expressed in a fear of monsters. But the question is: is that the
only reason Dave's fear has gone on so long?

*One thing Mark and Lisa know about Dave is that he is
not a generally "fearful" child. Indeed, he is quite adven-
turous. Mark has taken advantage of their new locale,
taking Dave on overnight camping trips in the mountains
and desert. One would think that a child who feared monsters would fear them even more in the wilderness and in
the dark. Not so. He loves it out there. The only place he
fears the monsters is at home.*

It seems, then, that Dave is not really so much afraid of
monsters as he is afraid of something else, and in all likelihood
it is involved in some way with his parents.

*When asked how Dave managed when Mark and Lisa went
out alone and he was left with a baby-sitter, Mark and Lisa
shook their heads—that never happened. They didn't go
out much, and when they did they took Dave with them.*

Now we have a better idea of what is going on. Dave is
being "used" by the family system as a kind of buffer between
Mark and Lisa; indeed, literally, at night, Dave would sleep
between them. Dave's fear of monsters, then, isn't something
that just concerns Dave; it's something that involves the family.
It's been latched onto as an excuse to focus on Dave and to keep
him between Mark and Lisa.

*Mark and Lisa weren't all that surprised that this is what
was happening in their family. Underneath it all, they had
an inkling that something else beyond Dave's fear of monsters was going on. Indeed, when asked what would happen
if Dave no longer feared monsters, they said they'd have
to face each other and deal with conflicts they had been
avoiding.*

This case history gives us an idea of the way family members are inextricably bound to each other. The family operates
ecologically—what goes on with one member affects all the
others. In the case of the Sawchuks there were many things
going on at once, to all of them. There was the move across
country, uneasiness in their new surroundings, new work pressures, as well as the basic stress of parenting a growing child.
All of these elements took part in sustaining what otherwise
would have been a normal, transient childhood fear.

This basically is what family therapy is about: it looks for
what sustains the symptoms, rather than what caused them.
The focus is on the connectedness of individuals, rather than on

their separateness. Family therapy concerns, as the late brilliant seminal thinker, Gregory Bateson, put it, "the pattern that connects." Several different schools of family therapy have developed over the past forty years, but the common goal of all of them is to work on families as systems, shifting the focus from the symptoms of an individual family member to the problems that exist in their system. The goal is to help families change, so that such symptom bearing (Marty is his family's symptom bearer, Suzy is hers, and Dave his) is no longer necessary for the survival and stability of the family. In this way, by correcting an existing limited and limiting arrangement of the family system, family therapy creates new opportunities and possibilities for growth of the family itself and the individuals within it.

Not every child's fear is sustained, for not every family is in a situation in which it needs to pick a symptom as some sort of stabilizer. Indeed, there are a good number of what we might call "healthy" families that cope very well with a child's fear, usually letting it run its own often transient course, with support and understanding.

The Healthy Family System

Healthy may seem like a loaded word to use when describing families. It is not, however, used in a judgmental way, but in a clinical manner, to describe families that function relatively free of symptoms; families in which the inevitable struggles of development and stresses are worked out in ways that don't become rigid patterns; families that deal with the vicissitudes of life in such a way that *everyone* grows. Healthy does not mean *good,* nor does dysfunctional mean *bad.,*

Although, as we all know, a family's public face is not necessarily the same as its private one, it wouldn't be hard to identify several such "healthy" families—we all probably know several, to greater and lesser degrees. But defining "healthy" further and determining exactly what constitutes a healthy family is difficult. The definition depends to a great extent on culture. In some cultures, obedience to familial authority and remaining with one's family throughout life is considered healthy, whereas here in North America, where separation and differentiation are highly prized, that is not the ideal.

In analyzing what appeared to be healthy, symptom-free families, researchers have discovered certain traits. One trait is the family's overall goals. In general, a healthy family in our culture has two primary goals: to support and aid in the development and socialization of children on the road to eventual independence, while at the same time nurturing growth in the parents. The continued growth of the parents, although sometimes overlooked in family study, is very important, for as a recent spate of books on the best-seller lists indicates, human development does not stop after adolescence, but continues throughout life. Indeed, in ways appropriate to their ages, children are also responsible for the growth and development of their parents, for example, allowing them to be together on occasion as spouses rather than parents.

THE MARRIAGE

At the core of the American nuclear family is the relationship between the two spouses, and for a family to function healthily the marriage must first be healthy itself.

And what is a healthy marriage? Beyond the basic ingredients of love, respect, and fulfillment, a healthy marriage is one in which the spouses share power basically equally, which doesn't mean they act equally at all times; one may carry the ball for a while and then the other. It is one in which spouses communicate openly and directly, share a level of deep intimacy without feeling vulnerable, are happy with their sexual relations, and have their own strong individuality, which includes interests and opinions the other may not share or agree with but nevertheless accepts. They will have shared and separate friends and confidantes outside the family. Spouses must recognize each other's strengths and weaknesses and be able to defer gracefully, and *they must be able to separate themselves from their own families.*

The importance of a healthy marriage is paramount. For one thing, children use their parents as models of behavior, and if they see mother and father bicker or keep silent or show little affection, and they have no other example to learn from (such as grandparents or aunts and uncles), then they may come to believe that's the way all marriages are and that's how they should behave when they grow up. The effects of poor modeling may become apparent in all the children's relationships as they grow up, or it may not become manifest until the children themselves get married or at the point they have children.

An unhealthy marriage can also produce immediate negative results by disrupting the family system. Children, who naturally see the family as a safe haven and source of security, react adversely to the disruption. What makes it worse is that children will, without knowing exactly what they are doing, often seek to intervene in the marriage troubles in one way or another. They may "act up" to distract their parents from their difficulty, or may feign illness (or develop it psychosomatically) in an effort to bring their parents together again, or protect one parent against the other's overt insults. At this point we would

like to make what may be to some a rather startling assertion—
children take care of their parents—not in the usual explicit
ways but by their behavior or, at times, other ingenious or
exasperating means. This disposition is rarely conscious but is
built into the family system, sometimes as symptoms. Parents
may long to be parented themselves and project onto their
children attributes of their own parents. Perhaps that is one
reason grandparents and grandchildren are often so close (they
may also have a common enemy—the parent).

POWER

How power is distributed throughout the family is another
important factor in the family's health. In families that work
well, parents have the power, commanding authority and respect. The children also command respect and are given autonomy appropriate to their age and stage of development. Parents
are always open to suggestion and compromise, yet retain the
power of final decision. This is not to say that parents in such
families are absolute rulers, but there is a hierarchy, and they
maintain what is called the generation boundary. Parents
should be parents, and children should be children, for with
power comes responsibility, and children should not, under
normal circumstances, have to shoulder such responsibility.
The family that works well is run democratically, with the
recognition that children's ideas may, in fact, be legitimate and
useful.

COMMUNICATION

The family's greatest defense against things going wrong is
communication. Good communication is a matter not only of

what is said, but how it is said, when it is said, and a recognition of who it is said to. In a troubled family, members may get their thoughts and feelings across to a degree, but it might be through the implications of silence, or sarcasm, or hurt looks and snorts of derision. Or the words may say one thing, but the tone, loudness, and setting may say something else, so the verbal messages become contradictory or confusing. The object is to promote communication that is open and direct between all members of the family—not just to say, but to have "it" heard in a meaningful way.

This does not mean that conversation has to be a model of eloquent language and parliamentary decorum. On the contrary, in families that are working well, communication is usually quite spontaneous, with members speaking whole sentences in a single nod or gesture and frequently interrupting each other because of their excitement at relating some idea. Yet though the manner and conduct may be somewhat freewheeling, the most important part of communication is always present—people listen to what others have to say. And important for the children, the communication, both talking and listening, is conducted at varying levels, depending on who is communicating and what they are talking about.

There are different depths of communication and it's best when members are able to use them all—when they can have an easy exchange of information or express their thoughts and feelings, all without any worry that they or their ideas will be discounted, rejected, or ridiculed. And every now and then it's important that they be able to dig down to the deepest levels of emotion to express dreams and hopes, fears and frustrations.

Although that deepest level of communication is not required often, the knowledge that it can be tapped into if needed gives the family strength and security. Family members feel safe, not vulnerable. They know they can express the most intimate and personal thoughts and feelings without fear of being humiliated or betrayed. And if a parent doesn't know the answer to a question, they don't feel challenged or humiliated but admit not knowing and convey to children the availability of others who do know or of books. Or they admit that some questions simply don't have answers.

Feeling secure and safe within the family isn't the only positive result of good communication. By allowing everyone to say what they think and feel, without worrying whether or not anyone else agrees with them, individuality is encouraged.

INDIVIDUALITY

Individuality is another key characteristic of families that work well. It's not just accepted, but actively bolstered and applauded. Family members must feel not only that it is acceptable to be different, to have different views and different interests, but that it's wonderful. The family should operate under the notion that through diversity comes strength. This isn't always easy. Because of the strong team atmosphere in a healthy family, there's a lot of incentive for each person to fit into the family image.

> *The Turners are an athletic family—Andy Turner is an ex-Olympic kayaker; wife Helen is a one-time regional figure skating champ; daughter Judy is a triathlete; and eldest son Rob is following in his father's footsteps on the white-water circuit. There is one more son, Jon, but he's not much interested in sports. He'd much rather spend a day working on his Apple IIc than go waterskiing. In other families he might be treated as an oddball, as the one who*

*doesn't fit in, but in the Turner clan he's been given a sort
of special status in the family—he's "the smart one."*

Fostering individuality is crucial in the drive to accomplish one of the primary goals of the family—raising children to be independent. One of the reasons it can be a difficult task is that it can be awfully hard *not* to live through a child. Parents often try to make their children what they wanted to be, but couldn't; thus the stereotypical, but often quite accurate, image of the "backstage mother," or the father who presses his boy into Little League.

FAMILY MYTHS

As the child asserts individuality, he or she will take a place in the family mythos. Each family has a collection of myths about itself. A common one is that Mother is the expert cook, whereas Father is lost in the kitchen. Or Father is a whiz in the garage, and Mother doesn't know a thing about cars. Or Mother is comfortable with feelings and Father is not. These myths often have only the slightest basis in reality and can have both a positive and a negative effect.

A positive effect is that they can encourage a child's sense of competence in certain areas—a little boy may be supported as the family musician, a little girl as the family comedian. The negative effect is that these family myths can often be stereotyped—as in the case of Mother-in-the-kitchen and Father-in-the-garage—which can be limiting and may indicate deeper, more rigid roles, for example, Mother nurtures and Father is remote. They can lead to self-fulfilling prophecies. They also may lead to a loss of self-esteem when reality doesn't conform to the myth. In healthy families the correct balance is struck.

The myths are, in themselves, generally positive ("Jill is a good athlete"), rather than negative ("Dad can't balance the bankbook"). Most important, the myths are not rigid, but flexible and open to a rewrite.

ROLES

At a deeper, more fundamental level than family myths are the roles that family members play. To use the analogy of a play, family myths are like the character descriptions of a part given in the text (John is the comedian in the group; Julie is the intellect), whereas the *roles* that people play in their families are like the function of the characters in the play (Laura takes care of her friends; David is the catalyst for disruptive change).

Each member of the family should play many roles at the same time, or at least be capable of it. Within the family a woman often plays the roles of wife, mother, friend to husband, lover, friend to child. Children are offspring and siblings, as well as friends of parents and siblings. There are also roles that are not defined in terms of relationships (mother to son), but by the character of the function (care giver and provider) and roles that relate to the outside world (worker, volunteer, student, friend). The roles of parents and children change as they grow, especially children, as their experience in the world broadens and expands. The less mature children are, the fewer roles they play (primarily because they have fewer contacts with other people, contacts that define new roles).

All is well when each role fulfills a needed function in the system or in relation to the outside world, and each person is "right for the part." In families that aren't working so well, when trouble arises it's often because role playing has become skewed, either because the wrong person for the role takes over the part (voluntarily, involuntarily, or without even knowing it), or because the role played is one that would not be necessary if the family were functioning healthily, or when one role obscures all others.

One kind of inappropriate role playing occurs when children assume roles that are parental in nature, such as care giver or nurturer. When this happens children, in effect, start parenting their parents. Or a child may create or be unconsciously coaxed into taking on a new and negative role, such as family troublemaker or peacekeeper. Why would a child take on such roles? It's usually not a matter of choice, but rather the family system's attempt to stabilize a deteriorating situation. The child may act precociously and may at first even enjoy it (there is some satisfaction in "taking care" of someone who's supposed to be so much more powerful than you are), but in the long run it's highly disruptive, and sadly, in the bargain, the child has to give up some valued aspect of being a child, such as time to play or the sense of having a mature and competent parent.

Stability may be achieved through this skewed role playing, but it comes at high cost—a status quo of unhappiness and discomfort—and it is a precarious and unsteady solution. It's as though one were trying to save the sinking foundation of a house by driving in wedges and propping it up instead of by pouring a new foundation.

The goal is a situation in which the roles played by each person reflect reality (parents are parents and children are children) and are appropriate to each person's abilities and stage of development. There is also flexibility. It's not as though once you're the baby in the family you should always be the baby (although that is often the case). As each person ages, there is movement from role to role, and in families that are working this movement from one role to another is not merely tolerated and accepted; it is enjoyed and encouraged.

But these characteristics of a "healthy" family—happy marriage, shared power, open communication, realistic myths, appropriate and changing roles—are not the only factors distinguishing a family that works from one that doesn't. There are those traits that characterize the structure of the family system that point up how the system works or does not work.

Traits of the Family System

The family system is an extremely byzantine and complex organization. There are countless unwritten rules and regulations that lay out how family members are to deal with one another and the outside world. On this systemic level, families that work and families that don't have profound differences. These could be called the traits of the system.

FAMILY ATTITUDE

Perhaps the most basic difference is the family's general attitude toward life. Just as families tend to have a particular ethos (athletic, intellectual, academic, blue collar), so they tend to have a particular overall attitude. In general, healthier families tend to be optimistic, whereas families at the other end of the spectrum tend to be pessimistic.

This does not mean that healthy families are blithely Pollyannaish, or that pessimistic families wake up thinking each day will be doomsday; it's just that families that work take a more positive view of life. They expect things to turn out for the better, rather than for the worse. They view humans as essentially good or at least modifiable creatures who usually make mistakes for reasons of duress, and they are not usually afraid of strangers or of new situations.

Families that are not making out so well tend to take the opposite tack. They do not look positively at new situations, are distrustful of strangers and predict things will get worse rather than better. To them, it's not so much that humans are evil, but rather it's our nature to look out for ourselves first; all others are a distant second.

It's not hard to see how this basic difference in attitude can color so much of life, even when not in the extreme. Pessimism affects not only how these family members see the outside world, but how they see themselves as well. There tends to be less openness, less communication, and less of a sense of family closeness and togetherness.

It might seem that an optimistic family would be more prone to suffer when things go wrong in their lives, such as death, unemployment, frustration, whereas a pessimistic family, ever prepared for the worst, would fare better. But the opposite is true. A positive attitude allows a family to go on—they believe things will get better—whereas for a negative family, calamities and disappointments only confirm their predictions, adding to the negativity.

RIGIDITY AND FLEXIBILITY

Families that are not working too well are often characterized by rigidity—in terms of authority and power, rules and codes of behavior, channels of communication, and most of all, fear of change. From this comes the emphasis on stability at all costs; when things are not working well the instinct may be not to try to fix the situation, but just to stabilize it and stop it from getting worse. Indeed, a rule of thumb for rigid families is: if something doesn't work, do more of the same.

This is much like someone suffering from seasickness on a rocking boat who assumes if he can just keep still and not move he'll be fine. In the case of the troubled family, though, the boat is most often rocking, not from rough seas that are beyond the family's control, but because of turmoil from within—something they probably could deal with themselves.

In contrast, a family that is flexible and open to change is going to fare better. In such a family few problems get so out of control that the boat starts rocking hard in the first place; they see problems coming and face them before they get out of hand. And if the family boat did begin to rock, the first instinct of this family would be to look inward to see what was causing the motion and deal with that, as well as look outward for sources of assistance. In those cases where the rocking was caused by something outside the family—an external stress such as unemployment or illness—they would be able to mobilize the family's strengths and resources, including its supportive friends and relatives, to weather the storm and steady the boat.

In essence, a flexible family system is more likely to work better because it's better equipped to cope with the various stresses and changes that are bound to occur throughout life. A rigid family is not so well equipped. It meets different challenges with only a few, often inappropriate and tired responses. The defensive reaction of hunkering down and resisting or attempting to ignore the stresses from within or without may achieve stability for a time, but again, that time is limited and the stability precarious.

CHAOS AND CONTROL

At the other extreme are families that are chaotic. This poses other problems to the health of the family. Children thrive best in an atmosphere of security. They need a safe haven of protection from which they slowly can emerge as they get older and function more autonomously within society. Part of security is a sense of order and predictability. If the hierarchy in the family is disturbed (perhaps one child has been forced into taking a parental role), or authority is haphazard and rules are unenforced or unenforceable or inconsistent (as can be the case with an alcoholic parent), then chaos results, and the child is left foundering, trying to find his or her place in a structure that shifts and is unsteady. Role definitions are undelineated, unclear, and no one, let alone the children, is sure who should play what part, with parents and children switching roles. Children in these families may look outside for sources of security and sanctuary.

In the healthy family there is the pervasive sense that things are in control—not just in the control of the parents, but of the family as a whole. All have an idea of who they are and where they fit in.

OPEN AND CLOSED

Openness, although not so open that the family loses definition, is also vitally important. This has a lot to do with how the family communicates, both among its members and with the world around it. A closed family is one that is shut off from the outside world. It is insular and self-involved, unwilling to allow anything to penetrate its exterior. One obvious result of such sealing off is that the inhabitants of the closed family can suffocate.

The family is but one system, albeit the most critical one, in any person's life. Beyond the family system are relatives, workplace, networks of friends, affiliations. It is from these other systems, from the outside world, that a family receives the information and energy that comes from other people and new ideas. These resources help to prevent the family from getting "stuck," and they make for optimum problem solving. If the outside energy source is cut off, then the family has to be self-reliant.

We think of self-reliance as a virtue, and yet, in the case of a family that tries to be completely self-reliant, it can be a mistake. Think of a single living cell. Although it is defined and separate from all other cells, it also relies on cells outside itself for sustenance. If it doesn't get it, it dies. In the case of a closed family, without energy from outside, it grinds down, able only to feed on itself.

The other effect of being closed is that not only are communications with the outside world curtailed, but channels within the family shrivel and dry up. When the mind-set of the family group is such that they are "closed to outsiders," each member will become closed, not only to outsiders, but to fellow family members as well.

What may occur in such families is something called *enmeshment*. When family members become enmeshed, they are so "close" to one another that they lose a sense of themselves as individuals. They seem to think and act in unison, as a group. It may be hard to see where one person ends and another begins. The paradox is that these members are not, in reality, "close" at all. Indeed, there is no shared intimacy, no open communication of thoughts or feelings, rather, just a fear of being different.

All differences are suppressed out of deference to the

group. Each member is afraid to walk out of step, to be unique, for to do so would make him or her, in effect, an outsider. Such families are also characterized by invasive language—one person will tell another person what that other person is thinking or feeling ("You're sad"), what he or she *should* think and feel ("You're sick, go to bed"), or will generalize from his or her own thoughts ("I'm hungry, let's eat").

You have probably never met such a fully closed family, primarily because such families have very little social contact with the outside world—you might not even know they were there. But they do exist, and we do occasionally encounter such closed systems, but usually only on the eleven o'clock news. Consider this one:

> *This "family" was very close. They lived communally and were so enmeshed that they didn't even have their own names or identities. Feeling persecuted on religious grounds, they moved to South America to start a new life. But when they thought that the persecution had followed them, they performed the ultimate act of desperation together—they took their own lives. Dying from the same cause, at the same time, all believing in the same thing; nameless, faceless, undifferentiated one from the other. The leader of this "family" of 900 was the Reverend Jim Jones. The place was Jonestown, Guyana.*

Cults, such as this one, are the ultimate example of a closed system. *Beware of closed systems!*

BOUNDARIES AND DEFINITIONS

To return to the analogy of the living cell, although it needs the outside world for sustenance, its survival also depends on its being separate from that world. In the family, this separateness and individuality of each member is crucial for the necessary development in thinking, feeling, and behavior.

Similarly, just as each person, each "self," needs defined boundaries within the family, so the family itself needs a defined boundary within society at large. It cannot be completely exclusive, as it is with closed families, but there must be a sense of team spirit within the family, a feeling by all that they are part of a unique group, distinct and separate from all that surrounds them.

In contrast to families with defined boundaries are families with boundaries that are too permeable—systems so open that they lose any specific definition and blend into the background. There is no sense of belonging among the members and nothing that anyone can point to that could distinguish them from the crowd (except a shared name). They are a family in name but not in function. Every need becomes fulfilled from without. Children search outside the family for what should be available inside—love, support, belonging. Family members may have greater attachments to people or institutions outside than ties to those in the family.

TIME AND CHANGE

The way a family deals with the inescapable and inexorable reality of time and change is another clue to the character of its structure. Families that are working well regard the passage of time and all the changes it brings as being not only inevitable, but often welcome. Time and change do not merely signify aging and death, but growth and development. That isn't easy.

It can be hard to watch children grow up and, to a degree, away from the family. Yet, as hard as this can be, families on the right track aid and encourage such growth (for one thing, it allows parents to use it as an opportunity to explore and expand their own interests). And when it comes to the hardest realities of time and change to accept—aging and death—these families accept them and deal with them, perhaps searching for some wisdom from their encounters with both.

The troubled family, however, is characterized by an effort to ignore or forestall time, not just because of a fear of death, but because time means change, and change can disrupt the fragile stability of the family. The fear is that any movement could bring the whole thing down. In particular, there is likely to be a subtle or overt attempt to hold children back by denying the fact that they are getting older in order to keep them within the confines of the family.

COPING AND NOT COPING

Just as they can be distinguished by how they react to time and change, so families can be looked at in terms of how they cope with problems. The goal is for families to meet problems early and directly, to head off any magnification of the trouble. Open communication of thoughts and feelings is crucial, as is the ability to use outside help.

Troubled families, however, may attempt at all costs to ignore whatever is causing trouble for as long as possible. The hope is that if it's not discussed it might just go away, and the fear is that if it is talked about, it might get worse. Nothing could be further from the truth. Problems ignored don't disappear, they just get worse.

SOCIAL NETWORKS AND SUPPORT SYSTEMS

The extent of a family's social network and the quality of its support systems is perhaps the most telling barometer of health. They are important when things are going well, absolutely vital when things are not going so well. Indeed, the family's most important resource is its connectedness to the outside world— its ability to tap into support systems for help.

The phrase *social network* is a term of quantity; it means, in plain numbers, how many people a family has dealings with over a period of time. *Support system* is a term of quality—the people that could be called upon in a time of trouble.

In the diagram of a social network in Figure 1 we see that the family is at the center of a series of concentric circles. The people farther from that center, though having weaker ongoing relationships with the family, may be called upon in specific circumstances.

Dr. Gerald Caplan, a noted social psychiatrist, in a lecture some years ago, described seven basic categories of people that can go into being a part of a support system.

1. Relatives and friends.
2. Professional care (it has its limits in distance from the family—both mental and physical—as well as cost, and is available on its own turf, usually nine to five, Monday to Friday, by appointment).
3. Nonprofessional help givers (everyone from friends to bartenders: people the community regards as "good ears").
4. Nonprofessional specialists (cancer veterans, parents of drug abusing children—often people who have been through a specific trying situation and have made

FIGURE 1

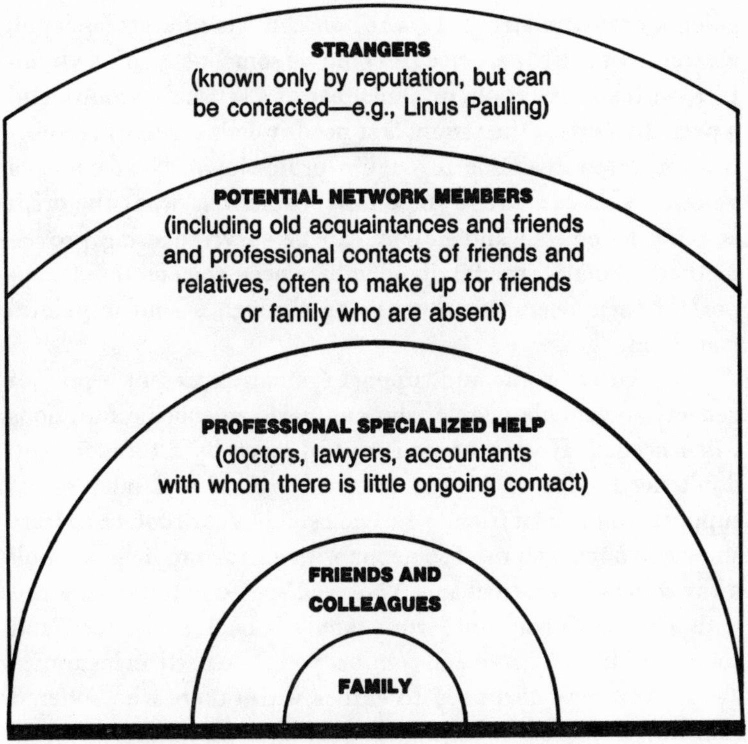

STRANGERS
(known only by reputation, but can
be contacted—e.g., Linus Pauling)

POTENTIAL NETWORK MEMBERS
(including old acquaintances and friends
and professional contacts of friends and
relatives, often to make up for friends
or family who are absent)

PROFESSIONAL SPECIALIZED HELP
(doctors, lawyers, accountants
with whom there is little ongoing contact)

FRIENDS AND
COLLEAGUES

FAMILY

themselves available to others going through the same
ordeal).

5. Specialized groups and foundations (e.g., Cancer Care,
Reach to Recovery).
6. Self-help groups (e.g., Alcoholics Anonymous, Al-
Anon).

7. Religious groups (both for calming rituals during predictable life crises and for various support groups).

The ideal support system for a family or individual undergoing a dramatic stressful *transition* consists of a professional, a veteran of the experience (it could be someone who's a volunteer, with a foundation, or a member of a self-help group), and a peer. In a crisis, the family first needs reliable, accurate information, often available through a professional. Next comes a veteran, who can advise the family, explaining what the crisis is going to be like and how it can be survived using proven methods. Finally, the family members need the emotional support of their peers or others going through a similar painful transition.

Social networks and support systems represent a pool of generally available people who can perform specific functions when needed. If your house is ripped apart by a tornado, you don't need a lot of friends to stand around and offer moral support; you need a friend who can rebuild your roof, or at least show you how. You need someone with a winch to help you pull away some of the wreckage. You need someone to provide you with a place to stay until your family is back on its feet, and someone who will listen and comfort you. You need an insurance agent. You may also need to gather with others who suffered similarly, because they, above all, provide an instant connection.

Ideally, a family should have tremendous resources, both in terms of raw numbers (a big social network, with each adult person in the family connected to another twenty-five to forty people) and in terms of quality of relationship (the support system should be broad and strong).

At the other end of the scale are families with very limited social networks and social systems. They will simply not have as broad a range of friends and associates to call upon when they need to. Nor may they have perhaps the most key element, reciprocity—the ability to respond to others in need as we would want them to respond to us. Therefore, the one-way nature of the attachment will inevitably overburden the helper and end up in burnout. A family that is closed may have a member with a serious psychological or psychosomatic distur-bance. This family organization, once again, is not causative. The illness may exaggerate propensities that are already there, or the interactions (and perhaps shame) within the family and help seal off the family from a viable outside network.

Indeed, a family may seem to be in fine shape—until it gets hit by something stressful, whether marital problems or a hurri-cane. The family's own internal resources will be severely tested, and once the resources have been depleted, if they don't have access to outside help, or are not willing to use it, they will be in trouble. They will be trying to face new problems with old solutions.

The world is confounding and we cannot know all that we need to know. Support systems provide information and re-source extensions of ourselves. With a support-system-impover-ished family, minor issues can become a series of disruptive crises that are otherwise mere perturbations in a support-system-rich family.

In general, many of the various traits of the healthy family's system seem paradoxical. On the one hand the system must be flexible to adapt to change; but it cannot be too flexible—there must be a feeling of overall control. It must be open so that it can receive information and energy from the outside world; but it must not be so open that it lacks a defined boundary to distinguish it from the outside world.

In truth, it is not that the family system is paradoxical, but, rather, that it lies between extremes: between rigid and chaotic, closed and undefined. The goal of the family is somehow to function dynamically and live between these extremes, between rigidity and chaos, between a closed border and no border at all.

It should be remembered that the model of the healthy family is in itself an extreme, that most families fall somewhere in the middle, going through periods of being relatively healthy and other periods of being relatively unhealthy. The question is: how is your family doing?

Identifying Problems

Having read this far, you now probably recognize something of how your own family operates. If you wish to have a more graphic picture of your family system, you may want to fill in the questionnaire provided below based on research into the nature and character of well-functioning families by Jerry Lewis, M.D., and colleagues. This is a diagnostic exercise, not a test—how your family is working is not a matter of competition. It could give you a better idea of the specific strengths and weaknesses in your family's system and how it is faring overall.

THE QUESTIONNAIRE

There are twenty-five statements listed below. To the left of each one indicate whether you agree with the statement, disagree, or aren't quite sure.

AGREE	DISAGREE	UNSURE

1. I am encouraged to be myself.
2. You have to watch what you say in our family.
3. We can take care of ourselves—we don't need any help.
4. We try to face problems and solve them early on, before they get out of hand.
5. Change makes us nervous.
6. Parents are interested in children's suggestions.
7. I don't want to be any different from the rest of my family.
8. We generally talk on the surface of things.
9. We all work well together, like a team.
10. We're all angry a lot of the time.
11. We all like to try new things.
12. Others in the family act like they know what I think and feel.
13. Sometimes we'll talk about our deepest hopes and fears.
14. We all look forward to meeting new people.
15. We're a rather emotional bunch.
16. There's one boss in our family.

AGREE	DIAGREE	UNSURE	
_____	_____	_____	17. I can freely express what I think and feel.
_____	_____	_____	18. It's a tough, dog-eat-dog world out there.
_____	_____	_____	19. Outsiders can't be trusted.
_____	_____	_____	20. Both parents share the leadership role.
_____	_____	_____	21. We don't like others to know how we feel.
_____	_____	_____	22. The others listen to me and make sure they know what I'm saying.
_____	_____	_____	23. We only deal with problems when they are absolutely unavoidable.
_____	_____	_____	24. There's a right way and a wrong way of doing things.
_____	_____	_____	25. We can always confide in one another.

THE RESULTS

Each response has been given a weight. Below are the statement numbers and the answer expected from a member of a better functioning family. This is always either an AGREE or a DIS-AGREE. Give yourself 4 points for every answer that matches the answer listed below, no points if your answer doesn't match, and 2 points for each statement to which you responded UN-SURE.

1. AGREE	6. AGREE	11. AGREE	16. DISAGREE	21. DISAGREE
2. DISAGREE	7. DISAGREE	12. DISAGREE	17. AGREE	22. AGREE
3. DISAGREE	8. DISAGREE	13. AGREE	18. DISAGREE	23. DISAGREE
4. AGREE	9. AGREE	14. AGREE	19. DISAGREE	24. DISAGREE
5. DISAGREE	10. DISAGREE	15. AGREE	20. AGREE	25. AGREE

Add up your total points.

INTERPRETING THE RESULTS

There is a maximum possible total of 100 points. The 100 point total was chosen purely as a matter of convenience and there is no percentage basis—a 78 point total does not mean yours is a 78 percent healthy family.

Indeed, this questionnaire has no real validity outside of what it means to you. We cannot say, for example, that 45 or 66 is the median, or 51 or 72 the average, nor would we want to.

The statements have been worded in such a way that they will not make you shy away from answering, even if it's the honest response, because it seems so negative. Therefore, you might find yourself disagreeing with the answer indicated as the healthy response.

For example, statement 15, "We're a rather emotional bunch," is shown as a healthy statement. The statement was worded to appear ambiguous, so that it would not seem either too positive to agree with it or too negative to disagree. Indeed, a person who disagreed with the statement could argue that "rather emotional bunch" conveys a sense of chaos and lack of control. However, families that are open with their emotions, that are able and willing to show when they are happy or sad, are usually healthier than families who are not so open. Therefore, since open emotion is generally positive, so is the statement.

In short, the questionnaire is designed to help you spot trends that could lead to trouble in your family system.

The overall trend is indicated by your total score, which most likely will fall somewhere on the line between the very healthy and the dysfunctional. There are no "good" or "bad" scores. It would be safe, however, to say that a score of 0 would be truly unfortunate, and a score of 100 would be straining credulity. Scores in the neighborhood of either extreme— within thirty points or so—would be the most indicative of the general health of a family's system.

The overall total is, however, not the real point of this questionnaire. The statements were designed with seven categories in mind—seven areas of potential trouble in a family system—that you can focus on.

Statements 6, 16, 20, and 24 are concerned with the nature of power and flexibility in the family. They are intended to help you learn whether the power is in the hands of one parent or, as in families that work well, if it is shared by both parents, and whether the power is used in an authoritarian manner or if there is some input from other family members into how things are done.

Five statements—2, 8, 13, 17, and 22—deal with potential problems of communication: is everyone made to feel that they can express themselves openly and directly, or do they have to watch what they say? Does family conversation stay at the superficial level of simple information exchange, or can it go deeper? And perhaps most important, do family members really listen to each other?

Related to communication are statements 1, 7, and 12, which are concerned with one's individuality within the family, and 10, 15, 21, and 25, on intimacy and security. Both are matters of support of autonomy and trust. In the healthy family, each member is not only allowed but encouraged to be different. Family members are also accorded their own space and identity—no one invades their sense of self with statements like "You feel tired, go to bed." These family members are also open with their emotions. They don't feel they have to hide them because they might be ridiculed; they know they can trust whomever they confide in. And though they are emotional, the predominant emotion isn't anger, for anger is something that breeds and thrives in silence and repression—when it is communicated, it tends to go away.

Five statements—3, 9, 14, 18, and 19—concern whether or not the family is open or closed, defined or without boundaries. The idea here is to attempt to discern the underlying family philosophy. The healthy responses to three of these statements—9, 14, and 19—are fairly obvious. Healthy families certainly do have a team atmosphere, and yet at the same time are open to new experiences, new people, and are not automatically afraid of strangers. Statements 3 and 18, however, are intentionally more ambiguous.

"We can take care of ourselves" sounds like a positive

statement of self-reliance. However, when coupled with "we don't need any help" it betrays the closed-off truth of the statement, the suspicion that something is lurking "out there." The goal is for the family to give and take with the outside world and be willing to use outside resources when the need arises, knowing that not every problem can be solved at home.

"It's a tough, dog-eat-dog world out there" is also ambiguous, for to many it would seem to be a reasonable statement, one that can be confirmed with a glance at the headlines of any newspaper. A family, however, shouldn't look at the world that way. The family that works well concentrates on the possible opportunities out there, not the possible disappointments. The cynic would scoff that such naifs are easy prey for the sharks of the world, but such is not the case. Families with positive attitudes tend to suffer no more and possibly less from stress than families who expect the worst, and they are better equipped to survive the stress because they see it as a temporary setback and not as a confirmation of the inexorable path to doom.

Statements 4 and 23 concern approaches to problem solving. Obviously, the healthy family is the one that works on problems straightforwardly and early, without letting them slide until they get way out of hand. Statements 5 and 11 show the healthy family to be open to new experiences and not afraid of change, for the fear of change often indicates an unhealthy, precarious, and stagnant stability in a family system.

Again, it cannot be overemphasized that this questionnaire is not a scientific test, but only a simple diagnostic tool to help you pinpoint the areas in which your family might need some work.

The Family System and Childhood Fears

In this chapter we have shown how family therapy theory approaches problems. It does not focus on one individual and search for the one cause of his or her problem. Rather, it looks at all problems in terms of their connectedness to the world around them and concentrates on the most important context in almost everyone's life—the family. Family therapy theory does not seek to blame or focus on one individual, but rather on the system.

We have seen what can go wrong in the system and how a family that goes off track can function in a way that perpetuates the problem rather than solves it. For example, the family system may sustain a childhood fear rather than let it pass. When a fear is sustained in this way, it usually will be found that child and parents have become involved in a self-perpetuating *triangle* relationship. Indeed, as we will see in the next chapter, the triangle is the primary clue to what might be wrong with the system.

3 Identifying Triangles and Their Meanings

If you look closely at any two-person relationship, you will see that somehow, some way, there is almost always a third element involved, especially if there is any conflict or stress between the two. Norman J. Ackerman, in his book *A Theory of Family Systems,* gives this example: "Challenge any well-functioning couple to go to a crowded restaurant with poor service, sit at a small table face to face, and see how long they can engage one another without getting angry at the waiter, commiserating with the waiter or one attacking and the other defending the waiter." And this doesn't occur only in restaurants, with waiters as the third party. The couple can be at home alone. If they are stressed, the third thing they focus on can be anything from their work to a television show. By bringing in this third element they expand from being just a couple, or *dyad,* into a *triangle.*

Why do triangles occur? According to games theory, they come out of our need to win: we're always seeking to form a coalition with a third party so we can gain the upper hand on our opponent. We're always looking for what in basketball is called the "two-on-one."

But advantage seeking isn't the only reason we form triangles. As we've discussed, systems are, to a degree, self-regulating as they seek a level of stability, and triangling is a self-regulating device. The major element it regulates is distance or closeness between two people. When things are good, the couple can maintain their closeness or intimacy but when there's some kind of stress, some kind of conflict, they, without thinking, will often draw a third party into the situation, either to keep them apart without totally breaking contact, or to unite them against the third party. The third party modulates the amount of distance and intimacy.

How does this work? Colleagues Drs. Jane Ferber and John Schoonbeck have provided the following example. Imagine three people circled by a loop of rope. If two of the people move away from each other they pull on the rope and the third person is pulled in between them, keeping the two people apart. Or if the third person pulls away from the other two, the couple will be drawn together. In this instance, the third party is used as a distraction.

Either by keeping the couple apart or drawing them together, the third party provides a "way out" (usually unconscious) for two people unwilling to confront each other directly over their conflict because they don't want to rock the boat; they're afraid of pain, awkwardness, and most of all of risking the basic relationship. Meanwhile, according to Ackerman's example, the waiter is across the room taking another order, oblivious to his role in keeping this couple together. He is lucky.

Obviously, this third item in the triangle, whether it is the weather, the waiter, or a movie, is treated basically as an object by the conflicted couple. If it is indeed just an object, or some unrelated and unwitting person, then the only harm done is that the couple is avoiding their problem. Unfortunately, in the case of the family, the third corner of the triangle is usually occupied by the weakest, most vulnerable member—a child.

Again, we are using the model of the two-parent family in this book, since one way or another, there is always a second person of authority, even in a single-parent household. That "parent" might be a grandparent or other relative, or it might be the other parent, now separated or deceased. Often, it is the oldest child (which can cause trouble, since acting as a parent is an inappropriate responsibility for a child). When there is stress there is always some "person" in that third corner, even if that person isn't physically there or even if that "person" isn't even a person (a child can be triangulated between his or her single parent and work or religious preoccupation or drugs or alcohol or something as amorphous as "the school system").

Like the oblivious waiter, the child (and parents, too) may not know what's going on, that there is a triangle (or, if aware, doesn't realize the full extent of the situation). Unlike the waiter, the child will not be able to separate from the couple at the end of the evening. The child has to live in the triangle, and the triangle is the structure that is usually at work in the family when a child's fear is sustained long past its normal life.

A warning: there's a temptation to see this triangling in a linear, individual-oriented, cause-and-effect light. We may say, "Aha! Parents, unable to resolve their own conflict, pull apart, drawing the child in between them, transferring their stress in one way or another onto the shoulders of their child, using him or her to keep the family and their marriage going." If one is looking for a culprit, however, one can also point a finger at the child; he or she is the one who, afraid of instability, jumps in between the parents to act as a referee, or acts out or gets sick to draw the parents' attention away from their conflict.

Again, this temptation to assign individual blame must be avoided. The parents are not at fault, nor is the child. It is a systemic problem. It is an earnest, well-meaning, if unconscious effort to deal with a difficult situation. In truth, to return to the image of the three people in the loop of rope, the problem is with the rope.

The Unhealthy Triangle

There is nothing wrong with a triangle. Indeed, when not too intense or restrictive and not sustained for too long, a triangle can serve many useful purposes within the family. A triangle only becomes pathological—sharply deviating from what is healthy—when indeed it does become too intense, lasts too long, is too rigid in its formation and becomes an enduring part of the family organization.

The basic unhealthy triangle can usually be found in a closed, enmeshed family where there is a troubled marriage. Unwilling or afraid to confront the problems between them directly, or even oblivious to them, one parent attempts to cross the line dividing the generations to form a coalition with a child. This gives the child a role—that of a parent's peerlike friend and close confidant—that is inappropriate.

The consequences and repercussions of this cross-generation coalition are serious and far-reaching. First, it further disrupts the already troubled marriage by essentially raising the child up to the level of parental status. This pushes the other parent out of the way, usurps his or her power, and breeds strong resentment. It also disrupts the relationships between the siblings—brothers and sisters resent the high status of the newly empowered child—and, potentially, among the entire extended family.

Most of all, it has a profound effect on the child who has been drawn into the triangle. The youngster may enjoy the newfound power of having pseudo-parental status for a time and may even cultivate it, but eventually he or she will resent the intensity and invasiveness of the coalition and will resist it, sensing that the precocious role is undertaken at the expense of normal enjoyment of childhood.

To complicate matters further, once one parent has crossed the generation line, it becomes easy for the other to do so as well. The parent on the outside of the coalition may make some attempt to draw the child away and into another coalition. The child in this position has few choices, none of them appealing. An alternative would be the other parent affiliating with another child in the family, thus resulting in the parents "dividing up" the children through a kind of US-USSR mutual escalation process.

For example, if a young girl tries to be good to both parents, or at least neutral, she will find herself with divided loyalties, trying to serve two bosses. It is impossible to stay in the middle, but as soon as she veers toward one boss, she is seen as being disloyal by the other and so pulls back in that direction. The child then starts to bounce back and forth, from one to the other. Potentially, in a severely troubled family, with a very intense, warring triangle, the child, not knowing which parent to believe, which one to obey, indeed, which one to love and be loyal to, can be immobilized by the quandary and will withdraw completely.

Sometimes the triangle involves three generations, as was the case in the Rogers family. Five-year-old Josh became afraid of being kidnapped by a very nice, tall, dark-haired woman—a description of his father's sister, who had recently moved to another city. Josh had been very attached to his aunt and was troubled when she left. In this family, the grandparents did more of the child rearing than the parents. A triangle had formed between the father and the son to gain the affection of the aunt, who was also the grandfather's favorite. The wife-mother was a depressed, withdrawn, figure; in this family, the action was centered on the father's involvement with his family of origin instead of his own wife and son.

It's no wonder, then, that cross-generational coalitions are so strongly prohibited in our culture. Indeed, many believe that the purpose of the incest taboo is not so much to restrict sexuality or prevent genetic defects due to inbreeding, but to enforce the line separating the generations, so that the governing dyad (the parents/spouses) is not disrupted and the child is not torn apart.

In all cultures, when there is trouble in the family, the line of conflict will always be drawn between the two members of the governing dyad, and when there's a split in the family, it will split down the middle of that dyad. What's interesting is that the configuration of the governing dyad is different for different cultures. In Western culture, as we know, the governing dyad is the husband and wife; in Africa, the governing dyad often consists of brother and brother; in Asia it's frequently father and son. In Hindu society the governing dyad is often mother and grown son, which means that it is threatened if a too intense relationship develops between the son and his wife.

The Healthy Triangle

Of course, not all triangles are unhealthy. Indeed, in most instances they are quite healthy. Morris Freilich outlined what he considered a healthy triangle, one consisting of

1. High-status authority,
2. High-status friend, and
3. Low-status subordinate.

In this triangle, a low-status subordinate forms a coalition with a high-status friend in order to counterbalance the power of a high-status authority.

Jason was having a hard time at school. His grades were slipping and he didn't seem to care. Not making matters any better was Mr. Bates, the principal. He was always hounding Jason—about his clothes, his marks, his "attitude." Jason would be long gone if it weren't for Mr. Orr, his English teacher. Jason can talk to him, he listens. Mr. Orr spoke to Mr. Bates and encouraged him to give Jason a break for a while, and he encouraged Jason to clean up his act. Things have been getting better.

Jason, of course, is the low-status subordinate, the principal is the high-status authority, and Mr. Orr the high-status friend. If we look for an example closer to home, a child in conflict with one parent may form a bond with the other (or with a grandparent or other adult relative).

In the family, the high-status authority is usually the parent who represents the instrumental instructor (the one who teaches the child the rules of life), whereas the high-status friend is the expressive instructor (the one who gives an emotional education). In previous generations this would have been divided along gender lines, with the father as high-status authority and mother as high-status friend, but today parents may alternate roles as they see fit.

Far from being harmful, this triangling is actually helpful. In such a healthy triangle, the child gets the benefit of alternating periods of instrumental, authoritative instruction with periods of expressive, permissive instruction. And having a high-status friend makes the child feel that he or she is not alone and powerless, and that there is someone working on his or her behalf in the higher echelons.

But, as you may have noticed, that is exactly the same configuration as the unhealthy triangle: a coalition between one parent and a child, at the exclusion of the other parent. Indeed it is. However, such a triangle does not cause problems if the status line, the generation gap, between parents and child remains intact and if there is an overriding positive relationship among the three and if the roles are reasonably explicit and acceptable to all (most of the time).

Although a coalition may be formed between one parent and a child, the parent's allegiance to his or her spouse is far stronger—just as Mr. Orr's ultimate allegiance is to the school's authority. In the family, the child is given some support, some power, but by no means is he or she raised up to the status level of the parents. Although they may differ on their approaches, and one may be more instrumentally or expressively oriented than the other, the parents' solidarity remains unwavering.

This healthy triangle can turn unhealthy if it becomes too intense and threatens to bridge the generation gap; if it becomes too rigid and inevitable; or if it occurs time and time again in the same manner and the players are not allowed the freedom to participate in other triangles in the family. If there is already trouble in the marriage, then the triangle might become unhealthy, since there is incentive for one parent to intensify the cross-generational coalition to the point of exclusivity.

If that occurs, the low-status subordinate starts taking the ever-increasing heat. Whether the child remains in the first coalition with the "friend" or also tries to please the "authority," he or she is in a difficult situation. In most cases, the conflict that is being played out through the child will escalate, in what has been called a mirror-image disagreement pattern:

if one parent gets more authoritarian, the other will become more permissive. Of course the child is not a completely passive player here. As the child's anxiety increases, he or she will act like a lightning rod to the warring parties, being more rebellious to the authority and more needy to the friend.

As the conflict escalates, the authority and friend will match each other, step for step, increasing the voltage. Many things could happen. The governing dyad, the marriage, could split in two over it (tearing the child apart as well), or the triangle could become realigned into some sort of dysfunctional balance that diffuses the built-up tension—the child could become "sick," or "bad," distracting everyone from the original conflict.

> *Gwen, age eight, has begun crying at school. It started a few weeks ago when her working mother, Andrea, broke her leg in a bus accident while going to work. She has had to recuperate at home, and each day Andrea has been at home Gwen has cried at school. The child is unhappy, anxious, fearful.*

If one looks only at mother and daughter, one might think that the problem lay in the child's sympathetic involvement in her mother's ordeal: Andrea is understandably shaken by the accident, so Gwen becomes fearful as well. However, this approach does not take into account the important contribution of a third person, husband and father Otto.

> *Otto has never been entirely comfortable with the idea of Andrea working. In fact, right now he's even a little angry with Andrea for being injured (if she hadn't been going to work this never would have happened). Andrea naturally doesn't appreciate this attitude—this is a time she feels she*

needs more support, not less. Of course, one reason Otto feels this way is he has always viewed Andrea as the backbone of the family, and he feels less secure with her incapacitated. This, then, is the conflict between Andrea and Otto, and that is where Gwen and her crying at school comes in. By crying and becoming fearful, the family's focus shifts onto Gwen and off the trouble between Otto and Andrea. This fragile, nonovertly angry equilibrium also keeps Andrea from returning to her now "dangerous" work, settling, for the time being, the entire family's ambivalence about her working.

As it happens, Otto and Andrea, although unaware that a triangle existed and that Gwen's crying and anxiety were playing such a role, nevertheless didn't allow the situation to continue. They first got over their feelings of anger and then worked on the conflict between themselves. By doing this, they took the onus off Gwen—she no longer had to distract them from their conflict with her crying—and so her anxiety disappeared. The situation could have been resolved in another way as well. If the school personnel had been able to calm Gwen down, they might have "detriangulated" Gwen, which likely would have forced Andrea and Otto to face the issues dividing them squarely or to incorporate another focus to maintain their avoidance.

Types of Triangles

Salvador Minuchin, a key figure in the field of family therapy, long ago noted that children were used by the family system to obscure or deflect parental conflict. In his research, Minuchin discovered four basic types of triangles that can be used to deal, circuitously, with strife: triangulation, parent-child coalition, detour-attacking, and detour-supporting.

TRIANGULATION

This is Minuchin's term for what we have presented as a basic pathological triangle configuration. In this type of triangle, the parents are openly at war—perhaps separated, divorced, or on the road to it—and both try to enlist the child into their ranks. This spells trouble. Each parent feels betrayed by the child's attention to the other, and the child is caught in the middle with divided loyalties.

> *The Fallis family is at war. If George says rain, Helen says sun. Unfortunately for young Alex, he's not allowed to say partly cloudy. George and Helen are vying for his attention like two ardent suitors, both accusing the other of trying to draw Alex into it—of course, the only reason they would say that is to appear reasonable and so get Alex on their side after all. Alex has tried being peacemaker, he's tried to ignore them, he's tried everything he can think of.*

If the Fallis marriage doesn't split apart with this type of intense, cross-generational, escalating triangle, then Alex himself might as a result of the anguish of trying to serve two conflicted masters. The harsh anxiety associated with his vulnerable, uncertain position can sustain a variety of anxiety disorders, including fears and phobias, obsessions and compulsions, as well as a last alternative, complete withdrawal from the "game."

FIGURE 2

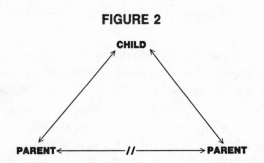

Triangulation: there's a war going on between the parents and they're both fighting for the support and allegiance of their child.

Since this triangle (see Fig. 2) cannot remain stable for long, it tends to evolve into one of the other triangles—parent-child coalition, detouring-attacking, detouring-supporting.

PARENT-CHILD COALITION

This is the fundamentally unhealthy triangle: a parent, seeking an ally or alternate attachment, crosses the generation and status-line boundary to form a too close coalition with a child.

Marge Houlihan and her daughter, Jill, are very close. They seem to be the best of friends, even though Jill is only five years old and has just started school. Marge needs a friend—husband Harry seems to be working later and later and paying her less and less attention. Recently, Jill has been having trouble going to school, as though she is deathly afraid of it, and Harry has been insensitive, sug-

gesting that he'll drag the kid to school if Marge can't handle it. (A good solution according to some professionals.)

In the case of this triangle it's hard to say who suffers the most—Jill, the child under pressure; Harry, the excluded and usurped parent; or Marge, a lonely woman—and impossible to say who "caused" it. Did a coalition form between Marge and Jill because Harry spends so much time at the office, or does he spend so much time at the office because Marge and Jill have excluded him from their group? Or did the triangle develop because a normal, transient developmental need of the child— her confused excitement about leaving home and going to school—elicits an overly attentive and receptive response from Marge? Or is the family unable to use a support system outside its boundary.

Again, this is a chicken-or-egg problem. In all probability there is unresolved conflict in the marriage, which, exacerbated by the child's developmental needs, is being expressed in the child's apparent school phobia, the father's spending so much time at work, and in the mother-child coalition.

The result of this parent-child coalition triangle (see Fig. 3) is that either the excluded parent or the child may exhibit exaggerated symptoms of distress, including anxiety-related disorders, such as withdrawal, phobias, compulsions/obsessions, hypochondria. Mr. Houlihan will soon be called an absent father, an unfortunately narrow and blaming label.

DETOURING-ATTACKING

This is Salvador Minuchin's term for the classic scapegoat triangle in which a child "acts up" and engages in "bad" behavior

FIGURE 3

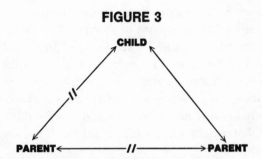

Parent-Child Coalition Triangle: the relationship between one parent and the child is strong, leaving the other parent out in the cold.

in order to distract the parents from the reality of their own unresolved conflict, which may be either a hot or a cold war. This can occur in an enmeshed, overprotective environment in which the child's symptoms help to provide some focus, structure, and stability for the family.

> *The Simons have always been a very close family that pretty much keeps to itself and takes care of itself. As such, Mr. and Mrs. Simon were completely unprepared when their son Terry, age seventeen, began skipping school, staying out late and raiding his father's liquor cabinet. And this behavior change seemed to come at the worst possible time—although they hadn't spoken about it, both Simons knew that there was some friction in their marriage. Now they haven't had time to worry about themselves as they've tried to get Terry back on track.*

Terry, without knowing exactly what he's doing, has sacrificed himself in this way to bring his parents together. He may think he's behaving poorly out of an amorphous sense of anger and frustration, or because he thinks he's "bad" and needs to be punished. What he won't consider is that he thinks he needs to be punished because, when he's punished, his parents are united, focusing on him instead of their own problems. Why now? Likely because his graduation and exit from the family is imminent, potentially forcing his parents with the stark reality of each other.

The interesting thing about this type of triangle is that the other members of the family, especially the parents, all usually seem healthy and are completely unaware that the problem could somehow involve them. Even if the parents had some idea that their child's behavior was distracting them, they might not realize that their child isn't acting on his own, but that his behavior has been implicitly supported by them, time and again.

The symptoms of a detouring-attacking triangle (see Fig. 4) are usually along the lines of behavior disorders—acting up, excessive aggression, tantrums, even criminal behavior. One trouble with this type of triangle is that it can remain stable for long periods of time, for although it is ruinous to the scapegoated individual, it does provide the whole system with a certain peace. However, the behavior problems this triangle encourages can escalate, as the more the parents try to crack down, the more the child rebels. This ultimately threatens the triangle, for at some point the cost of coping with the symptomatic behavior will outweigh the benefits derived from it. In that case, the triangle may come apart.

In most cases, however, these triangles are self-regulating—the parents battle; the child acts out to distract them; the

FIGURE 4

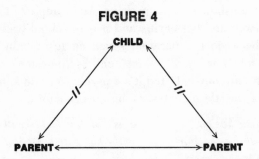

Detour-Attacking Triangle: the relationship between the parents becomes positive by default as the relationships between both parents and the "bad" child are negative.

parents unite against the child; the child, relieved that the parents are no longer battling, calms down; which allows the parents, now without their unifying cause, to start battling again—and the cycle continues.

In essence this is a balanced complementary relationship, with the parents on one side and the child on the other—as soon as one side is calm, the other acts up. But though the balance may suit the system, the individual child, sacrificed for the stability of the whole, is the one who suffers. His or her behavior is not just a way to distract battling parents, it's also a cry of protest.

DETOURING-SUPPORTING

Another way to detour the parents away from their conflict is to unite them, not against a "bad" child, but in support of a "sick" child. This produces a more balanced triangle, for all three relationships become positive. An example of this was the case of Gwen and her crying and fear of school brought on by conflict between her parents, which came to light when her mother broke her leg. The "sick" child's illness isn't always fear or anxiety, of course. Often it's a psychosomatic ailment, such as asthma, brittle diabetes, or bowel problems.

> *Darlene has had stomach pains and diarrhea recently. It's something the Harriman family has gotten used to. Darlene is the "special" daughter, the "special" sister, and everyone focuses on her to a degree. Not that it hasn't been an inconvenience. There has been some trouble in her parents' marriage this past year, which unfortunately has been a year that has seen an increase in the number of times Darlene has complained of stomach pains. The Harrimans have put off talking about their problems until Darlene is feeling better and whatever is the matter with her stomach is under control.*

As with detouring-attacking, the symptom-bearing child is almost always unaware that her illness may have come to serve a purpose. The parents are usually united in their concern and also unaware of the hidden agenda of the child's health. Even if they are aware that their child's illness is a reaction to their conflict—perhaps every time they start to fight Darlene complains of a stomachache and runs from the room—they will usually only think of it in terms of cause and effect (their fighting *causes* Darlene's stomach pains) rather than as a circular, systemic response.

In addition to psychosomatic illness, the symptoms of the detouring-supportive triangle (see Fig. 5) may also be learning problems (although not learning disabilities), social difficulties,

FIGURE 5

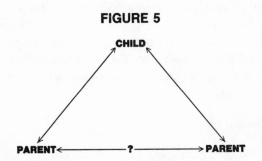

Detour-Supporting Triangle: the conflicted relationship between the parents is ignored or put on hold while they attend to their "sick" child.

or psychological disturbances—any problem that the child has had on a transient basis and that can be used as a distraction by the family. As with the case of Gwen, Otto, and Andrea, a problematic childhood fear can be used, because the whole family can rally around the child's anxiety. Of course, when the whole family rallies around the fear, it keeps it going and makes it harder for it to go away.

As with a detouring-attacking triangle, the detour-supporting triangle is relatively stable and self-regulating—parents fight, the child gets sick, the parents unite in support of the child and stop fighting, the child gets better, the parents resume fighting, and so on. However, the triangle need not remain stable. If the parental conflict escalates, the child's symptoms may escalate as well, to the point where their severity far outweighs the benefits of distraction they may provide.

Of course, at any level, for the child the benefits are

questionable, for the symptom-bearing "sick" child is under a considerable amount of pressure, in a position, a role, that is inappropriate and can easily distort the child's normal development. As with the scapegoated child, the symptom-bearing child's "sickness" is not just a way to bring warring parents together; it's also a protest against being put in such a position of responsibility.

Identifying Triangles

As was suggested by Ackerman's example of the couple in a crowded restaurant forming a triangle with their oblivious waiter, triangles can take many forms. The most common in the family is between two parents and one child. But if there is more than one child, there can be triangles among the children, between two children and one parent, and if the family is extended, with three generations present, then there can be any number of combinations of triangles involving grandparents, parents, and children. Indeed, in an extended family it is a grandparent or favorite aunt or uncle who plays the role of high-status friend for the child, giving him or her the feeling of having "a friend in high places." Of course, if it is too intense, or if it breaks down generational boundaries, this same triangle can also go off track.

Triangles, it must be remembered, are not the cause of the problem, but rather the structure that allows the problem to be maintained. Identifying the triangle usually provides the final clue to the puzzle of a family's distress. However, there are many triangles in place in a family at any given time and a search for one is likely to be confounding. Which triangles are important? Is one more important than another? A rule of thumb in systems theory is that a change in any part of a system can change elements in the entire system. This means that, to an extent, all triangles in a family will reflect each other, which in turn means that if you want to realign a family, to get it out of a rut, working on one triangle will have an effect throughout the family in all triangles.

Before one goes triangle hunting though, the first thing to look for would be ground in which unhealthy triangles could grow. One thing to be on the lookout for is the degree of connectedness or *enmeshment* in the family.

This degree of connectedness doesn't have to be anywhere near the extreme for there to be fertile ground for triangles—any amount of overinvolvement or overprotectedness can contribute. A sign of this can be a denial of privacy in the home shown by the opening, without asking, of doors and drawers, or a "no-closed door" rule, often including bathroom and bedroom, or secretly reading diaries.

Another sign is a couple that rarely goes out without the children (the excuse often is the inability to get or trust a baby-sitter). This *child-centeredness* in itself does not pose a problem. As an infant, the child has to be the center of attention—people have to act for the baby, think for the baby, or it will not survive. Even in later years, the child should be at the center every now and then so he or she can gain a sense of self-worth and importance. When this child-centeredness becomes too intense, however, when a child, by his or her actions, health, or behavior is controlling the whole family for long periods of time, then there is indeed a problem.

Of course, there are times when a child is particularly vulnerable, when he or she needs to mobilize and monopolize the family's attention for a while. After the crisis has passed, however, the healthy family is flexible enough to take the child out of the spotlight and resume as they were before. In the troubled family, things do not return to normal so easily. The pattern becomes rigid, long after the need for it has passed; for example, when parents continue to attend to their child's bodily functions—eating, defecating—beyond the point where the child could be expected to take charge.

If the child is at the center of the family and is, in fact, in control of it, then there is likely some kind of unhealthy triangle involving the parents. To identify the triangle, one would look for any cross-generational coalitions, either obvious or hidden, or other highly intense family relationships, positive or negative. One would also try to determine whether or not the child is participating as either a peacekeeper between the parents, or as a wedge, keeping them apart. Rigidity would also be a clue: are the same patterns repeated, time and again, with no one allowed to change or be different? A structure different from others described in this chapter may be seen in single-parent families, which now account for 26 percent of all American families. This is particularly true of single-parent families that are enmeshed in poverty. (According to a 1984 Census Bureau survey, 40 percent of single-parent families headed by white women and 60 percent of those headed by black women fall below the poverty line.)

In a family with only a mother and many children in the home, the parent may function inflexibly as the center of a wheel, with all communication going through her central switchboard and all control in her hands. There are no cooperative relationships among the children, who are not differentiated by age, precluding a hierarchy of power and responsibility. The older children do little to assist the younger. So much energy is expended in maintaining the family in the face of the chaos caused by the children's undifferentiated requests for attention that the mother has few connections beyond the family. Relief may only be obtained by "farming" the children out to other households. The woman fails as a mother, losing her only source of esteem. The children carry this pattern into school with similar demands on the teacher's attention. At least one child will exhibit behavior problems in school, and is generally the family scapegoat.

What to Do

The most important thing to remember is that although one child may have an illness that is running the family, the child is not the unit of interest; rather, the family is.

The problem with the traditional, individual-oriented view is that it tends to continue to isolate and focus attention on the symptom bearer, which can exacerbate the situation. The "bad" child is branded that way by society and his or her role is reinforced. The "sick" child is given special treatment and so continues to be special.

When it comes to childhood fears, if one just concentrates on the child who is suffering from them and ignores the context, the fears can be reinforced and gain in strength. As we will see, fears are not the product of an unhealthy triangle, any more than asthma is. But in certain situations, fears and phobias, which otherwise would pass in time, may well be the symptoms most readily suggested by the type of triangle and dysfunction the family finds itself in. Without understanding the fact that childhood symptoms can obscure serious issues in the family, removing the fear can precipitate an unmasking of the conflict. The family is not prepared for this consequence.

Unfortunately, it's not always that easy for a family caught in a web of triangles and unhealthy patterns to step outside of itself and see the state it's in. Usually, the main obstacle preventing a family from doing this is an inability to communicate openly and honestly. Indeed, in all situations, when a problem exists, whether it's between two people, the members of a family, or even the nations of the world, the first and most important step in solving the problem is simply to have the people involved talk about it.

4 How to Establish Effective Communications

Why is communication so important? For two reasons: it is vital to the person listening and to the person speaking. For the listeners, hearing what others think and feel lets them know what is going on, allows them to share in the lives of others, strengthening the bond between them; it's wonderful to trust someone with your feelings, and even more wonderful to know that you are trusted. Valuable information can be exchanged for problem-solving or corrective action. Open and direct communication, unlike restricted and limited communication, in which some subject matters are tacitly understood to be off limits, allows any problems that may surface to be dealt with quickly, before they have a chance to grow, unseen, beneath the surface. Misperceptions and misunderstandings, which often dictate and direct action, can be corrected.

Communication is also vitally important to the person doing the talking. First is the simple matter of being able to express feelings and vent emotions. In families where openness is not encouraged, emotions, especially the more negative ones, such as anger and resentment, may fester until they become true problems. Or the person may suppress all emotions so deeply that he or she loses access to them, even positive ones, such as love and caring.

The other important benefit of being able to communicate openly is a therapeutic one. Language is a tool we use to cope with the trials of life. Have you ever noticed how someone who has been in a car accident will often recount the story, again and again? By talking about it, one gains a certain distance from the event, a certain control over it—if it can be spoken, it cannot be that bad. (A catchphrase for this: "If you can name it, you can tame it.") The story of Rumplestiltskin illustrates the idea that if his name is spoken, he becomes impotent. Talking things over also allows us to sort things out. Language forces us to think a little more logically as we struggle to put feelings into words, and once they are put into words they can be looked at more objectively.

In general, good communication lays the groundwork for cooperation, problem solving, compromise, support, assistance, and comfort, all of which are important to the healthy functioning of the family.

Family Communications

Because we spend so much time with our families, certain patterns and processes of communication develop over the years, and how we communicate reflects what kind of structure the family system has. All families have unexpressed rules of communication. These rules, if limiting, can become ritualistic, whereas if they are open and generous, they can contribute to the health of the family.

PATTERNS

Much can be learned about how a family system is operating by listening to how the family members communicate. Consider how several families might deal with solving the same problem. In this one the son has been in a fight at school.

FATHER: *Well, Jimbo. Mom tells me you were in a fight at school today.*

DAUGHTER: *He beat the hell out of Ken Oag.*

MOTHER: *(to daughter): Ken Oag? (to son) You must have been awfully mad at this Ken to fight with him.*

SON: *He's just the biggest jerk in the world. He thinks it's real funny to trip people on the stairs. He tripped me and I really lost it, I couldn't help it. We started to fight.*

FATHER: *You feel good you got him back.*

SON: *Yeah, well . . . not really. I don't know.*

MOTHER: *You're confused. You don't think it was right, but you were angry.*

SON: *Yeah. But I feel . . . I don't know.*

FATHER: *Maybe a little uncomfortable. You don't like losing control.*

SON: *Yeah, I hated it.*

MOTHER: *I know what it's like. When someone cuts me off when I'm driving—*

SON: *What do you do?*

FATHER: *She takes it out on me.*

MOTHER *(laughing): I do not. It's hard. What do you think you should do?*

SON: *I think I better think about it some more.*

Their pattern of communication is one of open discussion in which the mother and father are looked to for guidance and direction, but everyone takes part in a kind of family debriefing. Notice the mother communicating her understanding by expressing her own (not her son's) feelings. The resolution came from the son—he needs to think about it some more. His parents don't feel any need for punishment; it looks like he's already been punishing himself. This pattern reflects a family in which the power is shared. Contrast that with a family where the power is not so evenly distributed.

FATHER: *Jim, your mother tells me you were in a fight at school today. What's that all about?*

DAUGHTER: *He beat the hell out of—*

FATHER: *I asked Jim—and that's no language to use at the dinner table. What happened?*

SON: *There's this big jerk. He thinks it's real hilarious to trip people on the stairs and—*

FATHER: *You fought him because of that?*

SON: *Not exactly. I—*

FATHER: *We do not allow fighting like that in this family. It's always best to walk away. After dinner I want you to do your homework, then stay in your room and think about that, all right?*

SON: *Okay.*

The discussion ends with a similar resolution—the son is going to have to think about what happened—but it isn't his choice. This resolution shows a family system in which the father, who obviously holds all the power, makes a weak gesture toward negotiation by bringing the matter before the family. At least in this family some sort of conclusion was reached even though there was almost a detour to the issue of what language to use. One could imagine that the resolution was a fait accompli, having proceeded in this "topdown" way many times before. Contrast that with a family where communication patterns are characterized by conflict.

FATHER: *So, Jim, you've been fighting at school.*

MOTHER: *Don't make it sound like it happens all the time. He hasn't been "fighting at school"—*

FATHER: *No? He got that bump walking into a tree?*

MOTHER: *That's not what I—*

FATHER: *Oh, I need this after I come home from work.*

MOTHER: *Will you listen. This was one fight—*

FATHER: *That's supposed to make it okay.*

DAUGHTER: *All Mom's trying to say—*

FATHER: *What? What is she trying to say?*

SON: *Will you stop this! It was nothing.*

MOTHER: *Nothing? You call that bruise nothing?*

FATHER: *That's great, son. You've made us both very proud.*

The family is in obvious conflict. The battle is primarily between the two parents, and the kids cannot help but be drawn into it. If the son acts out enough and turns his fight at school into something really big, maybe then the parents will stop their fighting and focus on him. Otherwise, the problem will not be solved. In fact, the two warring parents do not want it to be solved—they would rather fight over their child's behavior at school than deal with whatever is wrong with their marriage. In addition, everyone gets dragged in rather than just the principals. Chances are that all discussions in this family follow this inevitable, inexorable pattern.

Another route to a no decision is through denial.

FATHER: *How was school today?*

SON: *Uh, fine.*

MOTHER: *I told your father.*

DAUGHTER: *Everything's okay at school.*

FATHER: *You were in a fight? Nothing serious, right? Just a little schoolyard scuffle?*

SON: *Yeah.*

FATHER: *Thought so. Well, I know it won't happen again.*

MOTHER: *How was your day?*

Although the family hasn't denied that the boy was in a fight, they have done their best to treat the issue as quickly and superficially as possible. What they have denied are any possible implications of the incident—that the boy is having trouble controlling his anger, that he wants attention, that they might not be doing the best job of parenting. The trouble is, of course, ignoring a problem does not make it go away; it only makes it worse. What does one have to do to get attention in this family?

STYLE

We all know that often it is not so much *what* you say, but *how* you say it. Sometimes we'll receive a compliment from someone, but nevertheless feel uneasy, or we may receive criticism from a friend and for some reason feel encouraged. It all depends on how the comment is delivered.

Consider the drought-afflicted farmer who feels the first few drops splash on his face and says, "It's raining," as opposed to the Fourth of July parade organizer who steps out on her lawn, feels the precipitation, and says the same thing. Or consider the difference in message between the jilted lover who meets his ex-lover at a party and says, "You've lost weight," and the woman's physician, who, looking up from the scale, says the same thing. The first is a backhanded compliment; the second is a straightforward statement of fact.

A family's style of communication can be examined according to several different criteria:

1. *Clarity:* do people say what they mean, what they feel, or do they hide their feelings behind words and circumlocutions?

2. *Responsibility:* does the family's way of saying things imply that they blame others, outside of their immediate sphere of influence, for any misfortune that may befall them, or do they seem to take responsibility for themselves? Does one say, *"They* fired me," or *"I* was fired"? *"She* stopped too suddenly," or *"I* ran into her"?

3. *Approachability:* how easy is it to connect with another person for conversation? This is particularly important with children, for even if a parent doesn't have time to speak with the child, or is in the middle of

another conversation, it's important that the child know that he or she has been heard and acknowledged and that he or she will be listened to.

4. *Spontaneity:* in healthy families there is a level of excitement and enthusiasm that is apparent in how they speak. There are often incomplete sentences; conversation is vibrant rather than formal or stilted. These families are not like this all the time and can use more formal language when it is required, but in general, they seem to have fun.

5. *Invasiveness:* this is not so positive a characteristic. It involves a violation of an individual's or subsystem's (the siblings' or the parents') boundaries. A parent telling a child "You feel sick, go to bed," or "You're angry," or "I feel hungry, let's eat" is being invasive. Adults will not accept that; they will usually come right back with "Don't tell me how I feel," or "I'll decide when I want to eat." Children are not so independent. For them, invasiveness can be very destructive, eroding their sense of identity and autonomy. Development includes giving over the monitoring of a child's body and internal experiences to the child.

6. *Politeness:* the simple courtesies of conversation are important. Perhaps the most important is allowing other people to finish their thoughts.

FEELINGS

Expressing feelings is one of the most important aspects of communicating. In any given family, the family members may be allowed and encouraged to express all of their emotions, some of their emotions, or none of them. The level of expression allowed in a family is set by the parents. Children learn how expressive they can be from their mother and father (who, in turn, of course learned it from their parents).

It is not usually something that is directly taught, like addition or the alphabet—although a parent may, occasionally, tell a child not to be angry or so excited, or another may tell a child that it's okay to be sad or happy—but rather something that the child learns through observation. Do parents show affection to each other? Do they express their anger, sadness, or other negative feelings, or do they try to hide them? Do the expressed feelings seem out of sync with the behavior, expression, or body language?

In the healthiest families, parents and children alike are allowed to talk about any and all of their feelings, *with consideration of who the listener is—it's not a matter of anything goes.* The primary tool of expression is language, especially for negative feelings—parents will not encourage young Tim to express his resentment of new baby brother Chris by bopping him on the head with a toy, but they will encourage him to label the feeling and talk about it. Again, this is important because just talking about things helps. Telling someone you are angry with what they did brings the matter into the open and defuses the intensity of the emotion—as long as the other person is ready to hear it and can respond without being defensive or punitive. It's not easy, but it can bring remarkable relief for both people.

Some people might just shake their heads at this and say that the expression of all feelings simply shows weakness and a lack of self-control and discipline. But is that true? Consider the risks when a child is reared this way, told to keep all of his or her negative emotions in check.

Jane had been a "good little girl" all her life. Her parents had taught her, both expressly and by example, that nega- tive feelings weren't to be shown, especially by "good little girls." Jane kept her negative feelings to herself. She never seemed to get angry or upset, or become jealous or envious. Then, one day in her late teens, as she was about to go off to college, for no apparent reason, she was stricken with panic and couldn't leave her home. All she could do was cry.

For Jane, the lesson she learned from her parents was not simply that negative feelings should not be expressed, but that by extension those feelings are unhealthy. Of course, she didn't stop having the feelings, but when she did, she had to berate and punish herself.

Jane became angry at her mother, envious of co-workers, jealous of her boyfriend—all normal, natural feelings. But she felt tortured at having such feelings, because she knew they weren't "good," and so she was racked with insecurity and guilt that built to the point at which she could no longer handle it.

She was aware of the "hidden agenda" of her family's prohibition against negative feelings—there was a conflict be- tween her parents that they were unwilling and unable to ap- proach. Jane was afraid that if she left her parents alone when she went to college, they might express the hidden, forbidden hostility between them. And so she "sacrificed" herself by refus- ing to leave.

The suppression of feelings can, of course, have many different results.

John's father had been a career military man, a West Point graduate, who raised his son under the West Point doctrine that showing emotion equals showing weakness—the last thing in the world a soldier can afford to do. John didn't go into the military, but he did take this secondhand instruction with him. Now it looks as though John is about to become another statistic in the ever-growing number of divorces in the land. His wife claims emotional alienation and estrangement. John doesn't claim anything at all. He reaches for a drink.

Unlike Jane, who suppressed negative feelings, John has learned to suppress them all, negative and positive alike—he can't feel love or hate. If they try to erupt, he self-medicates himself.

The expression of feelings doesn't just help the person expressing them, it also helps the person listening. It teaches empathy, for when you find out that another person feels angry in a situation similar to one in which you feel angry, you learn a lesson of universality. You learn that you are not alone in the way you feel. In learning that, you may then be able to apply it to others when they show their emotions—you'll be able to say that you empathize, that you know how they feel. You are now more "connected."

Without the open expression of feelings in a family, family members can't learn that other people have feelings. Empathy is crucial, because it, along with trust, allows us to share intimacy with another person, and that is what is at the heart of any strong, close relationship. The key is that feelings are *just feelings* and there is a significant and important chasm between feelings and behavior.

LEVELS OF COMMUNICATION

The deepest level of communication is that of *intimacy.* But we don't usually get to that every day, nor would we want to—it would be exhausting, and besides, the fact that it is not something that happens all the time is part of what makes it so special and powerful.

The most superficial level of communication is that of *commonplace conversation.* This is the kind of chat we have with strangers in an elevator or, briefly, with an acquaintance at a party. It's the "lousy weather," "how about those Mets," "have a nice day" kind of talk. It may seem completely pointless and a waste of good air. But though the words themselves may be meaningless, the subtext of what is being said is far from pointless. Although it does reflect, to an extent, how we have learned to feel uncomfortable when there is silence between two people, it's also a way for us to make human contact, which helps us feel less alone and more connected, more a part of the human race.

The next level down is that of *straightforward information exchange*—"What happened at work today?" "We had gymnastics in gym class today at school." "Did you read in the paper about the bombing in New Zealand?" "I hear the Yankees traded for that relief pitcher." This level of communication satisfies both our need to talk about ourselves (which validates us as individuals and gives us a sense of self-worth and esteem) and our need to find out about other people. It also serves as an introduction, to see if more and deeper conversation can follow.

A deeper level of communication involves the expression of everyday *feelings and emotions*—"I'm really excited about this new project at the office." "Mr. Mellor is such a . . . He was really mean to this one girl in class today." "Mary and Tom moved today and I feel lousy." "Will you look at this baby? Is she the cutest child in the world, or what?" This level of communication allows people to vent their spleen, "get things off their chest," and enjoy themselves. It also helps build empathy, as family members learn how others feel and also learn the importance of overt encouragement and verbalized acknowledgment.

The deepest level is *intimacy.* That's when all the barriers come down and people express their hopes and dreams, their doubts and fears. It doesn't happen all that often and usually only between two people, although on occasion a few members of a family may share it at one time.

It is at this level that the wife confesses she always wanted to be a ballerina or a helicopter pilot and feels a little sad and unfulfilled that she never pursued it or she sometimes has bad feelings towards the kids. The husband says he has always worried that he was not attractive enough for his wife, or that his children do not think of him as strong or he wishes sometimes he could leave all responsibility. The daughter expresses her fears about not making it into a good college and disappointing her parents; the son reveals how insecure he feels around girls.

It is at this level that people feel true empathy, that they feel close and connected to another human being. It's the ultimate bond. It's where the isolation and loneliness that we all experience finally fades away, and we really feel part of the human race.

This deep level of intimacy is not something that everyone can reach all the time, nor is it, unfortunately, a level that all reach even some of the time. But in families that are working well, although it might not be used all the time, the possibility for using it is always there.

The capacity for such true intimacy varies from person to person, from family to family. Not everyone is able to reach down that deeply. People who do not do it may either question its importance or, like John and his father, see it as a sign of weakness and vulnerability. If there is one factor that may determine whether or not someone can reach this level, even occasionally, it is the degree of trust they feel. To be that intimate with another human being, you have to expose yourself and your vulnerability, and you will only do that if you trust the other person.

We learn much of our sense of trust from our parents. John did not just learn from his military father that it was imprudent to show emotion. He learned a much more destructive lesson—you cannot afford to demonstrate emotion because it shows weakness and will be exploited by your enemy. The need to avoid emotion in battle has been generated to *all* settings in his life.

Enemy? Who is the "enemy?" We return once again to the idea of overall family attitude toward life—does the family look upon their fellow human as an enlightened creature who likes to do good or as a base creature interested only in its own welfare? John's father probably raised his son the way he was raised—to believe that the other guy is invariably out to get you and to avoid being exploited, or worse.

Can John's marriage be saved? It's not easy to turn around the learning of a lifetime, but if John comes to realize that he can trust his wife and show his vulnerability, then maybe he will be able to begin to wake up his dormant emotions and finally achieve intimacy with another person. These are tough and complicated times for trust, but trust is essential, and good communications can help people achieve it.

When the Couple Communicates

Before parents worry about how they communicate with their children, they should give some attention to how they talk and listen to each other, for that is what children use as their model. They learn by observing how open their parents are, how they solve problems, how they praise each other, how they criticize each other.

If there is one basic tenet of good, effective communications, whether between adults or with children, it is that there must be both honesty and empathy. You have to say what you feel and yet be aware that what you say may affect the person you say it to.

Here, in no particular order, are some other tenets of good, effective communication:

1. Listen *actively;* this means letting the other person know you are interested by asking questions, getting clarifications, even by just nodding your head and saying, "I see."
2. Don't *do* anything. Active listening doesn't necessarily mean helping someone solve a problem. People will ask for advice and help when they need it; otherwise, what they're most often looking for is simply a sounding board.
3. Don't tell people what they're feeling; they'll tell you, if they want to. You can ask for clarification ("It seems like you're angry"), but don't presume to know what others are going through.
4. Accept responsibility for your own behavior. Basically, no one *makes* you do anything—someone does something and then you choose how you are going to

respond. No one makes you angry—they do things, and you become (even choose to be) angry.

5. Therefore, use "I" statements when expressing your feelings; instead of "You make me so angry when . . ." try "I feel so angry when . . ."

6. Remember, only seek to change another person's behavior if it bothers you, not his or her personality.

7. Don't try to change someone's behavior by coercion, punishment, negative reinforcement, or verbal abuse. Use only positive reinforcement. Minuchin has chapters entitled "Yes and. . . ." and "Yes but. . . ."

8. Separate the person from the behavior. It's not your husband you don't like, but rather his clipping his toenails in the bedroom. Work on that.

9. Start with some good news ("I like it when you do this") before you get to the bad news.

10. Define the problem specifically, without derogatory remarks, and define it in terms of yourself and what it means to you.

11. Express your feelings.

12. Admit to your role in the situation.

13. Be brief. Don't be encyclopedic, dragging in a whole litany of grievances; the idea is not to dredge up old hurts and wounds. Deal with one problem at a time, preferably soon after they occur.

14. On the other hand, don't try to resolve problems when you are still emotionally charged.

15. Joke about each other's strengths, not weaknesses.

16. Express affection and caring as much as possible.

17. Express praise and appreciation as much as possible.

18. Encourage each other often and support each other fully.

19. Spend time with each other just having fun.
20. Communicate often, remembering that good, effective communication takes time and practice.
21. Let only those involved in a problem talk, one at a time; if they get stuck, they should agree on calling in an additional person to try to resolve a stalemate or an escalation.
22. If you don't know an answer, admit it and seek reliable sources from experts or books and articles.

Parent-Child Communications

Good parent-child communications are of the utmost importance when it comes to dealing with childhood fears. What is your child afraid of? Does he or she feel open enough to tell you about it? Does the child have any idea why he or she is afraid? How can you reassure your children, provide them with the help they need to get over the fear? Answering all of these questions involves good, sensitive communications.

As with communications between adults, good communication with children is based on a "language of acceptance." This means letting your child know, by the things you say and the way you say them, that whatever he or she says or does, you accept the youngster. You are not going to judge, blame, or label your child. The paradox of this is, if you want your child to change behavior, you first have to let him or her know that your acceptance is unconditional, and you communicate that through what you say and how you listen. Only then, when the child feels accepted and secure, will he or she be able to change.

By contrast, judgmental or punitive responses will inhibit the chances of communicating further.

Contrast that with the effects of the language of unacceptance—parents telling their children that they are bad, period or bad for doing such and such, no good for failing at this or that. If children are told often enough that they are bad, or no good, chances are they will eventually start acting that way because there is no point in behaving any other way, and because it seems to fit parental expectations.

The most important thing to remember is to let children do things for themselves, whether it's building sand castles or working out a problem at school. This does not mean not helping—you must help, but only when asked to. When we talk about children crying out for help, most often the help they need is not some superparent jumping in to do things for them, but someone to listen to them, to understand them and to facilitate.

The language of acceptance has two major components—talking and listening.

The main we rèason we communicate with members of our family is because we have a problem that we feel needs addressing. Whether you need to talk or listen depends on who "owns" the problem. If the problem is something that is affecting your child alone—that is, it isn't causing any disturbance in your life—then your child owns the problem. Most often, when your child approaches you with something to talk about, it is because he or she has a problem that needs airing. In that case, you need to listen. If, on the other hand, the problem is something that is bothering you but does not bother the child—clinging to your arm, leaving toys around the house, coming home late—then you own the problem. In that case, you will have to talk.

LISTENING

As humorist Fran Lebowitz once noted, the opposite of talking isn't listening, it's waiting. Indeed, for most of us, talking comes fairly easily, but listening is hard.

Parents are often not the best listeners in the world. Many times they only give one ear to their children. There are many distractions, parents have many things to think about, and they may be tired. Actually listening to a child takes some time and energy, and parents can often be hard pressed to find much of either time or energy. But somehow they must.

Listening is the most important part of communicating. When you listen, really listen to another person, you tell them that they are important to you and that what they have to say is something that matters to you.

There are some keys to listening to your children properly. First, *be ready for it.* Make sure that your attention can be focused on the child. If you have something else on your mind, ask your child to wait until you are ready to listen and take care of whatever it is you have to do first. If you really want to watch the end of the news or finish reading a story, do so, but don't forget.

When you are ready to listen, give the child your full attention. Turn off the TV, put down the newspaper. Minimize any further possible distractions. If there are other people around, see if the child wants to talk privately. All of this indicates to the child how much you value this opportunity.

When the child starts to talk, really listen and pay attention. Remember the names of your child's friends, remember what happened the day or the week before, and solicit follow-up information on that. All this shows your child that you are interested in what he or she has to say and that it matters to you.

Your child will not always burst into the house with a story to tell. Many times you must invite the child to talk. Sometimes it is a good idea to set aside a certain time each day to talk; it need only be fifteen minutes or so. Ask questions of your child, be interested, but let your *child control* the course of the conversation, so that it's about what is important to the child, not what you think should be important to him or her.

Above all, remember that *this is not a time for instruction or criticism.* Even if your child says something that gives you pause, do not criticize it. You can always come back to it later, but you do not want to jeopardize your child's willingness to tell you what is going on and what he or she is thinking and feeling.

The way you listen to your child can take one of two routes. There is *passive* listening, where you sit back and with a few judicious "Hmms" and "I sees" let your child know that you are listening. Passive listening lets the child know that you accept what he or she is saying—you resist the impulse to respond and give your opinions. This is part of the first rule of the language of acceptance: do nothing.

You can also "do nothing" in a less passive way, in a way that will be much more fruitful for both you and your child. This is known as *active* listening.

At the heart of active listening is figuring out what your child is trying to tell you—what are the feelings behind the words that he or she is trying to express? Sometimes, though it may seem like your child is just relaying information, there most likely will be some hidden meaning to the story. Consider the story Randy, age eight, tells about coming home from school.

*The water was really rushing through this ditch and Barry
and I threw sticks in to watch them go. They went real fast
like they were little boats and then we stepped in to see how
deep it was and I was scared. It was real deep and I got
a soaker.*

Randy's mother's first response might be that she does not
want Randy playing near ditches filled with water, or that she
is upset that he got water in his boots and might get a cold. Both
are quite reasonable responses, but it is not the time for them.
Randy was scared and wants to express that. It is not the time
for admonishment.

Parents should *respond more to the feelings* than to the
facts of the story. Is their child happy, sad, fearful, angry? They
should try to figure out what it is their child is feeling, and once
they have, they can respond. But how to respond?

One could compile a long list of typical responses parents
make when their children tell them something, and none of
them, frankly, would be all that helpful. That does not mean
they are not understandable—far from it, they make perfect
sense—but they don't help the child or the situation.

First, there are those responses—ordering, lecturing, in-
terpreting, giving solutions, interrogating, moralizing, warning—that immediately cause the child to put up his or her
defenses. Children, just like all of us, do not like to be told what
to do, how to do things (especially if it is after the fact; for
example, a child stumbles and the parent says, "Be careful"),
or what they think and feel.

Then there are the responses that judge the child—name
calling, labeling, ridiculing—which are extremely nonproduc-
tive. Another unhelpful response can be withdrawal, using
humor as a distraction, which tells the child that the parents

are unwilling to listen or regard the communication as trivial. In fact, even being too supportive or praising a child can be counterproductive because it is beside the point; it's not what the child is after.

So, how do you respond while listening to your child? Either be noncommittal (the "hmms" and "I sees" of passive listening) or provide feedback. If you sense from what your child is saying that he or she is worried about a failed test, don't get upset that the test was failed, or urge harder study, but simply let your child know you sense his or her worries.

What the child wants in that situation is acknowledgment—*validation of feelings*—not guidance. By feeding back the child's feelings, he or she will know, not only that you are listening, but that you accept those feelings. And feedback is important to you too, for it allows you to check to make sure you were right in sensing what the child was feeling. Maybe you're wrong, and if you are, you'll find out, the child's feelings will be clarified and you'll be able to proceed.

How do you feed back? It's not simply parroting what your child says. If she says, "All the other girls have dates for the dance, but I don't," responding with "All the other girls have dates for the dance, but you don't" will probably elicit a puzzled look. Feedback is looking through the words to the feeling behind the words, and then putting that into your own words—something as simple as "That makes you feel bad."

A common criticism of active listening is that the parents' responses do not seem natural, not like the way people normally talk. To a degree they don't, but much of that changes when they're taken off the printed page and actually spoken. Most important in making it sound human is to share your child's feeling, be empathetic. You are not a computer or a psychoanalyst, you're a sympathetic friend who can think back to any time in your life to when you were scared, worried, or angry and remember how that felt. You have to really feel it. Children can sense fakery and phoniness very easily, and if they sense it, they will only feel condescended to.

Once you begin feeding back, let the child control the course of the discussion. There's no need for you to manipulate it or try to steer it in any way—children sense that just as surely as they sense any judgment or intervention.

Of course, intervention is the biggest temptation. You want to tell your child not to be afraid, not to worry, not to be so upset, to study harder. But parents should remember that they don't have to solve their child's problems. They don't have to give advice or make suggestions.

Most often, children and adults just like to talk, be heard, and be understood. *They usually want to solve whatever problems they have themselves* and would regard any attempt to help as intrusive. And as we have discussed before, just talking about a problem can help put you on the road to solving it. Even if it doesn't solve the problem, talking about it can reduce the fear and anxiety that is associated with it. Telling you he hates his math teacher probably won't "solve" your son's problem, but it will make him feel better about it. If your child does want help, he will ask for it.

Active listening can produce tremendous results for both you and your child, but it isn't easy to learn or use. And it has some rather stringent requirements:

1. You must want to help your children.
2. You must really want to hear what your children have to say, and you must give them your time and undivided attention.
3. You must be able to accept *all* of their feelings.

4. You must be able to trust your children to figure out solutions for their problems themselves, unless they request assistance.
5. You must remember that feelings are transitory and, if expressed, do not produce any lasting harm.
6. You must be able to view your child as a separate person, not just as a younger version of you.
7. You must be flexible and willing to face the possibility that by listening to your children without judging or intervening, you might see the world through their eyes and find yourself changed.
8. This process takes longer than a ritualized, same-old response and takes more creativity. It is inevitably a new one and requires a sense of newness in the listening and responding.

TALKING

When the problem is yours—something about your child's behavior has irked you—then you have to go to your child. You have to use the other component of the language of acceptance—talking.

As we noted earlier, *what* you say is often not half as important as *how* you say it. This is a vitally important concept to keep in mind when talking to children. Most often, the content of what you say to your child will either consist of praise or correction; therefore, your style of communication is critical.

Whether praising or correcting your child, first just simply describe whatever action or behavior you wish to praise or correct in as objective a manner as possible. The cardinal rule to remember here is that it is the behavior that is good or bad, not the child. Little Emma is not *bad* for smearing jam over the drapes, nor is she *good* for putting away her toys; smearing jam over the drapes is bad, putting away toys is good, but little Emma is good no matter what she does.

Language should not present love as conditional—"You don't want Daddy to stop loving you," or "Mommy will really love you if you do as I ask." If that happens, the child will have little self-esteem, as his or her entire sense of worth will be determined by the parents, which can lead to greater dependence and a severely diminished sense of autonomy.

After you have described the action, you should express your reaction to it (does it make you proud, angry, sad, happy?) and why you have reacted that way (you are proud because you are impressed by the accomplishment, angry because you just washed the floor, sad because it upsets you when your child is angry with you, happy because you like to see your child happy).

And of course you should acknowledge the child's feelings—does he or she feel proud, angry, sad, or happy?—and help your child try to figure out why he or she behaved in such a manner. There is no need to get too analytical; you just want your child to have some understanding of why he or she behaves in certain ways at certain times.

PRAISING YOUR CHILD

Praising your child is not simply a matter of patting him or her on the back. Praise is a way of giving instruction. The best way to do this is to be specific. Rather than saying, "Nice painting," it's better to indicate the specific things in the painting that please you—the colors, composition, control, or overall idea.

By sharing your feelings and reactions to what you think

your child does well, and by being specific, you let your child know what to expect from you, as well as what you expect from him or her.

Be generous with praise, but do not overdo it. Children are very perceptive. They often have a pretty good idea of the value of what they have done. They want praise on a level that is commensurate with their accomplishment. They get uncomfortable when praise is too effusive, or when it is generalized; they want to be praised for putting their toys away, not for being "the best little boy or girl in the whole wide world."

Above all, avoid backhanded praise, phrases like "I never thought you'd be able to do it," or "You cleaned your room— finally." This surfaces when there's something else going on in the parent-child relationship; perhaps you're a little peeved because you've been waiting all day for the room to be cleaned up, or maybe there is some lasting anger over a previous misdeed (or anger toward someone else displaced onto the child). But that should not be expressed when what you really want to do is praise your child as encouragement to clean up the room in the future.

CORRECTING YOUR CHILD

Children who are spoken to abusively often learn to speak abusively to others. Children who are given corrections without reason ("Why? Because I said so") tend to be less reasonable. Children who are spoken to sarcastically tend to use sarcasm as a way of communicating. Children who are not told clearly what is expected of them often do not know what to do.

The key to correcting your child, giving constructive criticism in a way that does not chip at his or her sense of self-esteem, is to use the language of acceptance. If you use accusing or attacking language, your child will put up defenses. None of us likes to be attacked, especially after we have done something wrong.

The first thing to do is to describe the situation as objectively as possible ("Your clothes are on the floor," or "You came home late without calling to let us know"). Then give your reaction, explain why you have reacted that way and why there's a need for a change ("I don't like it when your room's a mess because it makes it hard to clean and it collects dust," or "We get worried for your safety").

Next, you acknowledge the child's feelings ("I know it's your room and you think should be able to keep it any way you like, and you don't like me telling you what to do," or "I know you don't like feeling restricted by your parents and as if you have to check in all the time like a parolee").

The key to correcting children in a way that will make them listen to you is, as between adults, to turn "you-messages" into "I-messages." Frame your response, not in terms of what your child has done to you, but how you respond to your child's actions. In that way, "You make me so angry when you don't mow the lawn like we agreed" becomes "I get so angry when the lawn isn't mowed like we agreed."

If you think this is just taking responsibility for the problem, you are right. Remember, if your child is doing something you don't like, it is your problem—you own it. Your little girl is not upset when she writes on the wall with lipstick, you are. She did not make you mad; you became mad after seeing what she did. So, not only does reframing the reaction in terms of how you feel and not what they did keep your children's defenses down, it also makes sense.

It's important when framing these "I-messages" that you really express what is at the heart of your feelings. One emotion may be more dominant than another, but it is not at the root of what you're feeling. For example, it is easy for anger ("I get so angry when you don't call if you're coming home late") to disguise fear ("I get so afraid because I think something might have happened to you").

Finally, you have to give a clear indication of what you expect. "Pick your clothes up off the floor. Either hang up the ones you think you'll wear again or fold them and put them in your drawers. Put your dirty clothes in the laundry. This shouldn't take more than ten minutes. I'll come up to see you in half an hour." Or: "In the future you are going to have to call us. It doesn't take long and it doesn't have to be a big thing. We just want to know you're okay."

Don't overtalk or overexplain. Don't apologize. Both are often indications that the process is guilt provoking for the parent (just as overindulgence is such an indication).

We will not get into the question of what your reactions or expectations should be, except to say that, in general, your reactions and expectations should be directly related to the situation, should follow the behavior in as short a time as possible, and should be reasonable. In other words, you should not fume over a messy room for days on end, then explode, and then expect it to be as clean as an operating room within five minutes.

Whenever correcting your child, try not to overgeneralize ("Your room is *always* messy"), label ("You're just plain sloppy"), judge ("Why are you so bad?"), nag ("Have you cleaned up your room yet?"), give the silent treatment (it makes the child feel rejected and that he or she has no chance to explain an action and no chance at redemption), or make vague or violent threats ("Just wait till your father gets home," or "I'm going to knock your head off").

Children internalize what you say to them. In time, your voice becomes their conscience. How much better for the child's voice of conscience to be straightforward, observant, nonjudgmental, clear, understanding, and forgiving.

When the Family Communicates

In keeping with the perspective of this book, we should remember that good communications are not required only between parent and child, but between each member of the family. Indeed, as conflicts remain submerged in families because family members are unwilling or unable (due to unspoken family rules) to approach them, good communication between the adults is of paramount importance.

It is also important that every adult who communicates with the child use these guidelines. It should not be the job of just one parent to be the communicator. Indeed, there is risk associated with that. If one parent becomes the consummate listener and talker in the family, it may be at the exclusion of the other parent. It is possible one parent's skills at communication could be used to form a too close bond with a child, resulting in a parent-child coalition triangle. In fact, there is even some risk in both parents becoming too concerned, even obsessed, with "good communications" with their child, so much so that it becomes a distraction from them talking to each other and working out whatever problems they may have.

If we imagine the family that is working well for a moment, we can imagine all the aspects of good communications coming together. The family would get together at the dinner table. Their conversation would touch many levels—information exchange, a chance to perform and tell a joke, the expression of how family members feel and what they're thinking about, perhaps even touching the level of true intimacy. It would be a time of sanctuary for the family; a time for it, in a sense, to regroup and report back on what the family members had seen and done that day. It would be a time to look back and to plan for the future. Of course, the image of the family around the dinner table, as desirable as it may be, is probably antiquated as dinner is eaten either whenever each individual is individually ready or all sit together but face the TV set. The TV News has replaced the family News! That is unfortunate. It takes time to communicate, and families somehow have to find the time.

The Importance of Communicating

Good communications are tremendously important when it comes to coping with your child's fears. You need to know what he or she is afraid of, and you need to know why. Dealing with fears comes easily if good communications are practiced as often as possible; and not just when there is trouble, for it's likely that when there is trouble or stress families will fall back on the old, unhelpful ways of listening and talking. Helping your child get over his or her fears depends, to a very great extent, on your ability to communicate, both with your child and with other family members, to determine how your family is responding to the fear. As we will see in the next chapter, *what* the fear is—of the dark? of monsters? of cats?—is determined by your child's stage of development.

5 Fears That Are Part of a Child's Normal Development

Fear has served our species well over our several million years of evolution; it has been one of the keys to our survival. When we sense danger, the fear response kicks our body and mind into a kind of overdrive. Our senses are honed, our perceptions and vigilance sharpened; our bodies receive a rush of energy, preparing us either to run from the danger or to stay and fight. This is what happens when we awaken in the middle of the night because of a suspicious sound in another room or when, walking home late, we sense motion in the shadows.

But fear can also enslave us. It is such a physically and psychically powerful response that it can easily overwhelm us. This is important if we must dodge a speeding car or flee an attacker—we need to react, not think. But if the fear response is too intense and exaggerated, or if it is inappropriate to a situation, it can be disabling.

An example of exaggerated intensity is acute test anxiety. Most people have some anxiety about taking a test, and this is generally a good thing, for it can help them focus on doing well on the test. But if the anxiety is too intense, the sufferer will be so preoccupied with the anxiety that he or she will be unable to concentrate on the test and may do worse than he or she should have. Unfortunately, this experience in turn confirms and reinforces the initial anxiety, making it even harder the next time. An inappropriate anxiety would be an adult's fear of vultures, especially if the person lives in New York City.

Are *fear* and *anxiety* the same thing? The terms are often used interchangeably, and yet there is a difference. Fear is a response to a clear, present, and realistic danger, whereas anxiety is a more general state of apprehension that is unclear, unfocused, and unrelated to any present or realistic threat.

There are some problems, however, with that distinction. For one thing, both are "felt" the same way; they have similar physical effects on our bodies—sweating, racing heart, shortness of breath, increased vigilance—corresponding to an outpouring of adrenaline. And when does a fear become realistic or unrealistic? Is a fear of dentists, knowing that a visit can be painful, realistic or unrealistic? How about a fear of snakes, knowing that some can be poisonous? Here fear and anxiety will, for the most part, be used interchangeably, although fear indicates an intense response to a specific perceived threat, and anxiety describes an amorphous, unfocused apprehension.

To confuse the matter further, there is the term *phobia,* which is a combination of a specific fear and a current of anxiety. A phobia is an *exaggerated fear* that is out of proportion to the situation (for example, a fear of cats, which are not dangerous creatures) and *cannot be reasoned away,* even though the sufferer knows that it is irrational. A phobia will also cause an almost involuntary avoidance of the feared object, situation, or activity.

Although we have loosely defined these terms, we must realize that fear and anxiety are not "things." They are concepts, constructs, ways of observing and reacting. Fear is a state of mind and body, made up of several components.

There is the *cognitive* or thinking component—what we think when we are afraid: that we're going to die, or fail, or embarrass ourselves, or be injured. There is the *physiological* or bodily component—the sympathetic branch of our autonomic nervous system goes into high gear, raising our blood pressure, increasing our heart rate and breathing, drying out our mouths, dilating our pupils, and secreting adrenaline to give us a burst of energy (in some fear responses, such as fright at the sight of blood or injury, the parasympathetic branch of the nervous system operates in an exactly opposite manner, reducing blood flow and heart rate and causing some people to faint). And there is the *behavioral* or action component—flight, avoidance, and escape movements when escape is possible; shaky hands, stammering, and fidgeting if escape is not possible. All three of these components interact to produce the sensation of fear or anxiety.

The Origins of Fear

Is fear, especially a fear that we might consider unhealthy or inappropriate, something that we inherit genetically or something that we learn from our environment, especially our parents? The answer, as it generally is in nature-versus-nurture arguments, is that it appears to be some of both.

Child researchers (including the most inveterate child researchers of all, mothers) have long noticed distinct differences in temperament between even the youngest infants. Some are positive, outgoing, friendly, cheerful; others seem negative, shy, suspicious, fearful. It has been demonstrated by recent studies of identical twins raised separately that people are born with certain given personality traits that, combined with how they fit with their parents' personalities, set out some of the patterns for how that person will respond to challenges, cope with stress, and, in general, view life.

Of the various facets of personality that appear to be inherited, how an infant responds to new objects or people is the most important in terms of fears and anxiety. Some children will accept and approach new situations, whereas others, from an early age, will withdraw and fear them. There is evidence that these character traits may persist throughout one's life.

One study of a group of children found that some were timid almost from birth, and many of these timid children had a high, stable heart rate. Some of the children overcame their timidity over time, but none of them were among those with the high heart rate. Another study, of twins, found that if one identical twin had an anxiety disorder (such as a phobia or panic attacks) there was a 50 percent chance that the other twin would as well, but the correlation between fraternal or nonidentical twins was less than 15 percent. The general feeling is that a propensity for fears and anxiety can be inherited (specific fears, however, are not passed down genetically).

Fears and anxiety are also the product of learning and environment—the nurture element. Fears can be learned through classical conditioning, a theory holding that a response can become associated with one stimuli, as in Pavlov's experiment with dogs who associated the ringing of a bell with getting food and began to salivate in anticipation of the food whenever they heard a bell ring.

Another famous classical conditioning experiment, mentioned in the first chapter, was conducted in 1920 when eleven-month-old "Little Albert" was conditioned by researchers to fear a furry white rat—they whacked a frighteningly loud gong whenever he approached it. Eventually Little Albert began to fear any furry white object whether it was a ball of cotton or a Santa Claus beard. The second half of the experiment was to demonstrate how Little Albert could be counterconditioned and relieved of his fear of furry white things. Unfortunately for the experimenters, and Little Albert, Albert's mother took him away before he could be counterconditioned. No one knows what became of him and whether or not he feared furry white objects for the rest of his life.

Classical conditioning, however, does not appear to be how all fears are generated. For one thing, efforts to replicate the Little Albert experiment have shown that children are not easily conditioned to fear just anything—furry objects, yes, but not geometric shapes or a pair of opera glasses. We also know that not all things condition all people—almost everyone has had some pain in a dentist's chair, and yet not everyone has dentist phobia. Neither can every phobia be traced to a traumatic conditioning cause—snake phobia is quite prevalent and yet few people have been directly traumatized by an encounter with a snake.

Classical conditioning is not the only way learning and environment can generate anxiety. Fear can also be observed and learned through instruction. Children imitate their parents in countless ways, including what they fear—they learn that Mother is terrified of mice, or Father cannot stand heights, just by observing how their parents react in certain situations.

They can also be taught these fears by instruction—a parent or teacher tells a child to beware of spiders and snakes because they are dangerous. They can also learn these fears from movies (remember how reluctant many people were to swim in the ocean the summer *Jaws* came out?), TV, books, and newspapers (notice how the AIDS epidemic has created an epidemic of fear among some people beyond the legitimate and appropriate alarm). And yet, just as not everyone who has a traumatic run-in with a bee fears bees, not everyone who observes or is instructed in a fear develops that fear.

Interestingly, learning itself seems to have a genetic element, for though genetics only determines susceptibility and not specific fears, we learn to fear some things more naturally than others—for example, snakes rather than electricity. Up to 40 percent of the population has a less than positive attitude toward snakes, which, although potentially dangerous, are creatures few people ever come in contact with. On the other hand, few people are phobic about electric outlets, which we come in contact with all the time and know are very dangerous. It seems that fears of heights, deep water, snakes, storms, spiders, blood, injury—all fears that could certainly have served us well in our more distant evolutionary past—might be something that we are born somewhat susceptible to, and so we may be more disposed to fear them than equally dangerous objects of the modern era.

The other theory of the origin of fears and anxiety is Freud's which we touched on in Chapter 1. Freud argued that anxiety disorders were caused by an imbalance in the continuous struggle of the ego (our sense of "I" and "me" and its connection to reality) to balance the demands of the superego (essentially our conscience, society's rules as learned from our parents) and id (the instinctual biological desires for pleasure, often considered to be a release of bodily tension).

According to Freud, if the ego is too weak and the id too powerful, the id impulses toward pleasure and aggression, in conflict with the superego or conscience, are repressed, only to appear in another way, often as a neurotic fear or phobia.

Freud also felt the struggle could go the other way: if the superego is too strong and strict, then a person may suffer from a different form of anxiety, what he termed "moral anxiety."

Freud also coined the term "free-floating anxiety" to describe a state of general, unfocused anxiety that is the result of the ego's continual fear that the id's impulses toward society's forbidden pleasures and aggression will be followed and the person will act them out.

Finally, we should consider the systemic aspect of fears and anxiety. As with the genetic aspect of fear, it seems that glitches, hassles, or stresses in the family system do not cause specific fears or anxieties. Warring parents do not directly lead to a child's fear of bats, nor does a parent-child coalition lead directly to a fear of the bathtub; rather, the glitches may predispose a member of the family—the child caught between warring parents or in a parent-child coalition—toward developing fears and anxiety in general. Or as is more commonly the case, the child's normally transient fear, which may have *developed* for a variety of different reasons, may be conveniently sustained at that time by the family system in order that other, more painful issues be avoided.

It seems, then, that no one thing *causes* fears and anxiety. There appear to be a number of factors that come together (inherited, learned, and psychodynamic) to produce fears and anxiety, and others (systemic) to sustain them.

Fear and Anxiety Disorders

Many of the most prevalent specific fears are experienced by a great number of people, to varying degrees, from moderate (apprehensiveness about speaking in public), to severe (avoiding all social contact because one is afraid to speak). What is the difference between a normal fear and an abnormal one, where do we draw the line between healthy and unhealthy? As a general rule, a fear is unhealthy when through its intensity or persistence it interferes with what a person normally would want or need from life. (If someone afraid of flying never wanted to travel anyway, then such a phobia would not be a problem; although one has to be sure this is not just avoidance denial, like the child who, afraid of the water, denies any interest in swimming.)

An unhealthy fear is also irrational, and although the sufferer may realize that it is irrational, he or she cannot be talked and reasoned out of it. It is also likely to make the person want to avoid or escape from the feared thing, situation, or activity. An unhealthy fear will disrupt a person's life.

This idea of disruption is important—a woman who is terrified of flamingos, even though she lives in Nebraska, where she's unlikely to encounter one, is not necessarily phobic; *but* if that fear makes her afraid of going outside because she might see a pink plastic flamingo stuck in a lawn, then the fear is disrupting and limiting her life and is a problem.

Persistence is also important. A fear may be disruptive, but if it is short-lived the problem is minor. Most fears do disappear over time, although they can persist. And though many have their start in childhood, they can appear at any age.

Just how prevalent are anxiety problems? One study of a group of children over a twelve-year period determined that roughly 90 percent of them had, at one time or another, a fear that could be considered a problem. Another study found that although most childhood fears do, indeed, vanish over time, as many as 40 percent may persist into adulthood. But that does not mean that they are all disabling or disruptive fears. One study concluded that roughly 40 percent of the population have specific fears, 7.7 percent have true phobias, and only 0.22 percent have disabling phobias.

Following the basic lines of the American Psychiatric Association's *Diagnostic and Statistical Manual III,* anxiety disorders can be divided into the following types: specific phobias, social phobias, agoraphobia, panic disorder, generalized anxiety disorder, and obsessive-compulsive disorders.

SPECIFIC AND SOCIAL PHOBIAS

The term *phobia* comes from Phobos, a Greek god who soldiers would call upon to frighten their enemy (panic, by the way, comes from Pan, the mischievous prankster of Greek mythology who would terrify poor shepherds out of their wits with capricious practical jokes). Phobia was first coined to describe a fear by Roman physician Celsus, who in describing a fear of water (an effect of rabies) came up with the word *hydrophobia.* Since then, phobias have been named by taking the Greek word for a thing, situation, or activity and tacking *phobia* onto the end.

Specific phobias are often clustered into groups: animals; blood, injury, and illness; natural and supernatural (see Table 1 for some specific phobias).

An *animal* phobia, whether focused on dogs, cats, birds, spiders, mice, fish, frogs, or kangaroos, usually develops in childhood and rarely later in life. There is a certain amount of biological preparedness associated with such phobias—we are more likely to be afraid of snakes, which are more insidious and harder to spot, than, let's say, elephants. There is also the psychodynamic element—snakes may be symbolic of genitals. Animal fears usually go away as one gets older, but they can persist.

TABLE 1
Some Common and Uncommon Phobias

COMMON PHOBIAS

acrophobia—heights
arachneophobia—spiders
astraphobia—lightning
belonephobia—needles
brontophobia—thunder
catagelophobia—ridicule
claustrophobia—confinement
hemataphobia—blood

kakorrhaphiophobia—failure
musephobia—mice
nyctophobia—night, darkness
ophidiophobia—snakes
ornithophobia—birds
traumatophobia—injury
xenophobia—strangers
zoophobia—animals

UNUSUAL PHOBIAS

aurophobia—northern lights
ballisophobia—missiles
barophobia—gravity
dextrophobia—objects to the
   right

erythrophobia—the color red
harpaxophobia—robbers
levophobia—objects to the left
siderophobia—stars

Animal phobias are usually circumscribed; that is, the person afraid of dogs will fear only dogs and not all four-legged creatures. These phobias are generally not that disruptive and don't usually require treatment. They can become disabling and may require treatment if the fear intensifies and extends so that, like the hypothetical flamingo-phobic mentioned earlier, the person becomes so afraid of encountering the dreaded animal that he or she essentially becomes housebound.

The *blood, injury, and illness* group of phobias includes any fear that, at its core, involves injury or dying, a fear of disruption of bodily integrity, and a loss of body parts. For example, both fear of flying and fear of dentists would come under this category. The fear of illness can often lead to hypochondria and will often follow the current most notorious illness (it used to be syphilis or tuberculosis, for a long time was cancer or heart disease, then herpes, and now AIDS). This category also includes fear of injections, a phobia that usually peaks before age ten and then diminishes.

The specific fears of blood and injury are two of the most fascinating, for the physical response they induce in people who suffer from them is unique among the phobias. Most phobias induce people to escape the feared thing or situation if they encounter it. Blood and injury phobics, however, may freeze or faint at the sight of blood or injury. Instead of the fight-or-flight energy rush that accompanies other fear reactions, with these phobias a person's heart rate and blood pressure drop rather than soar, and fainting is common. Interestingly, this response is very phobia-specific—people who suffer from it are not more likely to faint in other situations—and is often prevalent in a family, although whether it is inherited or learned is unclear. What is clear is that it seems to be a remnant of an early survival tool—if one is injured and bleeding, a sudden drop in blood pressure and heart rate will reduce blood loss.

Fears of *natural and supernatural* phenomena usually begin in childhood. Monsters, witches, ghosts, and goblins quite often terrify young people over a period of few years, beginning around the age of three or four and ending usually before the seventh or eighth birthday as the child comes to realize they are not real threats. Fears of natural phenomena—lightning, storms, heights, deep water, darkness—also usually subside with age, although they may persist.

Fears of natural phenomena seem to have a lingering supernatural element—what hideous beast lurks in the dark?

What evil serpent resides in the deep water? What monster causes thunder and lightning? And when fears of natural phenomena persist, part of it may be a residual fear of the unworldly, despite the fact that the person knows it doesn't really exist.

Social fears usually begin in adolescence, although they can start as soon as a child begins school and begins to fear being observed, judged, or ridiculed. Anticipatory anxiety—the fear that builds as one anticipates encountering the feared situation—plays a big part in these phobias. People who fear an upcoming test or public speaking assignment will connive to avoid it at all costs.

Agoraphobia is almost exclusively suffered by adults. It is the most pervasive, disabling, and complex of the phobias. Its name—from the Greek for "marketplace"—is a bit of a misnomer, for it is not just fear of the marketplace, nor fear of being in open, public places. It is, in a sense, fear of everything. Typically an agoraphobic will suffer an acute panic attack when away from home. Wherever that happened—on a bus, in a church, on the street—becomes potentially anxiety producing. As the person suffers more attacks, the number of safe places narrows until the only safe place left is the home.

What the agoraphobic really fears, however, is not the marketplace, or the street, or the bus, or the church—but the attacks, which can make the sufferer feel he or she is having a heart attack, losing control, or going insane. In truth, what is feared, to borrow from Franklin Delano Roosevelt, is fear itself.

Somewhat akin to agoraphobia are *panic disorder* and *generalized anxiety disorder*. Panic disorder usually begins in the late teens. It is characterized by acute, unpredictable, inexplicable attacks of panic anxiety that leave the afflicted shaken, but essentially the same as before. However, there is increasing anticipatory anxiety because the attacks come unpredictably. Generalized anxiety disorder can begin as early as the mid- to late teens. It is characterized by a relatively stable, continuous, elevated level of anxiety, punctuated by occasional peaks of intensity without known situations triggering them.

Obsessive-compulsive disorders are included by some in the anxiety disorders, since they involve irrational and inappropriate fears. Obsessions are thoughts, images, ideas—usually of a morbid nature—that one cannot get out of one's head. The person will become obsessed, in a phobic way, about filth, disease, doing harm, seeing horrifying images, being embarrassed, acting out impulses. Compulsions are repetitious acts performed in a ritualized manner; they can also involve phobiclike fears, such as compulsive hand washing because of a fear of germs.

Any of these anxiety disorders can afflict children, although some are more likely to than others. In the next section we will look at the most common childhood fears and how they relate to a child's normal development.

The Fears of Childhood

It's not easy to determine exactly what children fear. Most studies of children's fears are based on the reports of parents. Although parents may be the most logical source of this information, they are not always the most reliable. If parents already have their own fears, they may color how they judge their child's fearfulness ("Is Jimmy afraid of snakes? Of course he is. Snakes are disgusting").

There is also evidence that parents generally report fewer

of their child's fears than would the child. This may seem strange in light of parents' usual overreaction to physical problems, but it is understandable when one considers the difficulty of seeing things from their child's perspective ("Is Jimmy afraid of ghosts? Why would he be? They're not real"). Sometimes parents just don't know. Some fears I elaborated in the introduction were not known by my parents.

Some patterns and trends of childhood fears can be discerned. Girls tend to be more fearful than boys. This could be viewed as inherited—an evolutionary survival tool, to make the childbearer more attuned to dangers to the nest. It is, however, just as easily explained by socialization—the persistent attitude that girls are more fragile than boys, the fact that girls are warned about dangers and are encouraged to fear things more than boys, and that they are also allowed to express their fears more openly than boys. This suggests that boys are just as afraid as girls, but they have been told to be brave and so they suppress their anxieties. Perhaps these anxieties appear elsewhere in a different form. Indeed, boys do outnumber girls when it comes to problems that have a potential for emotion and anxiety involvement, such as bed-wetting and stuttering.

In childhood, fears follow a general path, with certain fears usually occurring at specific ages and not at others. Although this is true throughout life—for example, fear of death usually increases throughout adulthood, peaking at about age sixty, then tapering off—the connection between age and fear is nowhere as strong as it is in childhood.

This is because fears, like the rest of the child's thoughts and emotions, are determined to a large extent by the stages of development, and though one's development continues until the last breath, at no time in life is that development as intense and concentrated as it is during childhood. Children may not have the cognitive wherewithal to understand all phenomena— i.e., perhaps some fears come from the poignant effort to understand complex perceptions with a "simple brain" and the inevitable misinterpretations and distortions that result.

The growth of the child's thinking and language capabilities determines what is likely to be feared. As the thinking becomes more abstract, so will the fears. Things a child never imagined could be frightening before—because they were beyond the youngster's ability to imagine—now become terrifying. The dark, previously just a lack of light, now harbors lurking monsters. Animals, once just seen as things, now are shown to have wills of their own.

Not only do new fears arise when the child can begin to conceive of them, but old fears disappear the older the child gets—what is frightening at five months (loss of support, loud noises) is not scary at four years of age, and what scares a four-year-old (creatures of the imagination) won't be frightening at age ten.

Fears are also determined by the child's expanding world. As an infant, unable to move, a child's world is small and the potential threats are few. As the child crawls, then walks, more of the world and its dangers are brought into view. And when the child ventures off to school, the number of stimuli that could produce fear grows astronomically. Not only do they change in quantity, but in quality as well, for it is then that the child becomes exposed to social pressures, and with them social fears.

A child's fears and the development stages associated with them, can be loosely grouped into three phases: infancy and toddlerhood, preschool and early school, and middle school and adolescence.

INFANCY AND TODDLERHOOD

Fear reactions are recognizable as early as the first three to four weeks. Loud noises, sudden bright lights, pain, and loss of support—all can cause a baby to show the startle response, stiffen, make unfocused movements, and cry. These are essentially diffuse, emotional reactions—something like instinctual or reflex responses.

They reflect that first stage of a child's development, in which the world is one of undifferentiated sensation. The baby has no true sense of fear, for at this early age there is no sense of self, no sense of action and consequence. A large component of fear is the cognitive process in which the individual speaks to him or herself. At this early stage there is no individual and no speaking, even in the most figurative sense.

True fears really begin as the child begins to think and form a concept of self as something different from the surrounding world. With the first true human fear—fear of strangers—we see the intriguing give and take between fear and development. Fear of strangers marks a major step in the baby's development.

For the first six months or so, the baby will generally respond the same way to everyone. Slowly but surely, though, the baby begins to sort out the images and begins to be able to pick out the primary caretaker—usually the mother. With the discovery that the mother is different from other people, the baby figures out that other people are not mother—and these people are not so welcome. Except for those in the immediate family (father and siblings), the baby may suddenly become shy and afraid even of grandparents who visited only a few weeks before.

Does this first fear simply accompany an important stage

of development, or is it directly caused by it? In this instance, it seems merely to accompany it; that is, the fear is not an automatic result of the newfound ability to distinguish one's mother from others. There is the matter of temperament (some children are inherently more fearful of new people and objects than others) and the matter of learning and environment (a child may have a traumatic encounter with a stranger, or may pick up contagiously, perhaps through overprotection, the parents' fear of strangers).

Fear of strangers does not last forever; it has its developmental limits. As a child comes in contact with more and more strangers and sees that they mean no harm, this stranger anxiety will usually begin to fade. In most cases, it will be mostly gone by the age of three or so, although in many of us a slight sense of apprehension at meeting people we do not know can continue throughout life.

Stranger anxiety usually ends sometime in the second or third year, but it can persist and become what is known as *avoidance disorder,* which is essentially acute shyness. A child with this disorder will be reluctant to engage in any new social contact and will retreat into the family. This can obviously impair the child's normal growth, stunting social skills and functioning and restraining the formation of, if not preventing, peer friendships.

Separation anxiety is another fear that marks an important, related stage of development. This usually begins sometime around the end of the first year, when the child starts to gain what Piaget, the brilliant child intellectual development theorist, called a sense of *object permanence.* To the young child, when something is out of sight it's out of mind—he or she ceases to think about it. To Piaget, this was both a matter of memory (the child of seven months simply lacks the ability to remember things on a short-term basis) and a matter of mental construct (the child does not understand that there are things beyond self that have an independent existence).

The child's ability to grasp this idea of independent existence and object permanence begins with the recognition that the mother is separate from everyone else. But even then, that is more a matter of memory and conditioning—a few faces, and one in particular, indicate a relief of displeasure, whereas other faces present an unknown quantity. It is when the child builds on this, with more experience and an improved memory, that it begins to realize mother has an existence unto herself. The child retains a mental picture of her. She is separate and she has permanence.

Paradoxically, however, the child's newfound understanding of the world does not yet include the ability to predict accurately future events from evidence from the past. As far as the child knows, when mother walks out of the room, she ceases to exist and will never come back. So the baby becomes anxious at any separation and will crawl after the mother, from room to room, just to make sure she's still there.

In this case, it does seem as though the fear—separation anxiety—*is* directly caused by the new stage of development, rather than just being an accompaniment. The two are inextricable. Separation anxiety does not just mark this stage of development; it is part of it. What makes matters confusing for parents is that another part of this developmental stage is negativism.

This is the other side of the child's learning object permanence—realizing that other things exist independently of him or her leads to independent thinking, and this, combined with efforts to forge independence, aided by newly developed muscular control, results in a certain amount of obstreperousness. The two types of behavior are paradoxically entwined. The child wants independence and yet is afraid of it and toddles back to cling to mother. The child fears separation, yet resists parental control and wriggles out of a hug.

Like stranger anxiety, separation anxiety does not last forever. Over time the child's egocentric view of the world will begin to erode as he or she begins to learn the principle of cause and effect and, from repeated experience—mother's inevitable reappearance after she disappears—that certain things can be predicted from certain events. Understanding language also plays a part in dispelling this anxiety as the child comprehends what Mom means when she says she'll be back.

Separation anxiety can, however, persist beyond the point at which it should cease, and it can become a real problem. Separation anxiety as a disorder is characterized by almost incessant clinging on the part of the child, refusal to go to sleep because it means separation, and, later, a refusal to go to school. The child will panic at any separation and will use psychosomatic illness to stop the separation. If the separation is forced, the child will be preoccupied with fears that harm will come either to self or parents.

At the point at which separation anxiety becomes a disorder it is no longer related simply to cognitive development. The child understands the concept of cause and effect and yet, unfortunately, is unable to apply it to the parents. For some reason, trust has been lost, and the child does not assume that when a parent leaves, he or she will return.

This loss of trust can be caused by a variety of circumstances. It can be internally systemic (a problem from within the family system, such as divorce when one parent leaves, making the child feel abandoned) or it can be the result of a catastrophe (death of a parent or a prolonged hospitalization for either parents or child).

In both cases the separation is very real to the child. There are three stages of reaction. Initially the child *protests*—with crying, tantrums, disobedience, clinging, which are all basic separation anxiety reactions. When the separation is not relieved, the child *despairs,* becoming quiet and withdrawn. After that, the child seems to return to normal functioning again, when actually he or she has entered the stage of *detachment* in which the youngster resists any reattachment for fear of being hurt again. Here is where the damage is done, for there has then been an erosion of trust.

Though both stranger and separation anxiety are developmental in nature and both usually pass with time, there are, obviously, potential pitfalls associated with them. Of the two, separation anxiety is the most potentially problematic in the long term, since it continues, in different guises, into the next stage of development.

PRESCHOOL AND EARLY SCHOOL

Separation anxiety appears in this phase in the form of school and death phobias. The term *school phobia* is a misnomer, since the child is not really afraid of going to school as much as of leaving home. Most children experience something of this reaction—leaving the home and going out into the world is a tough adjustment—but it is out of control if the child refuses to go to school or in some way manages to avoid it and gets the parents to acquiesce.

As an excuse, a child may say there is a threat at school (a bully or a mean teacher), or on the way to school (a big dog barking in a yard), or he or she will come down with a stomach-ache in the morning before school. Of course, none of these claims can be discounted; they must be checked out first to see if they have any basis in fact. But an illness in the morning before school is likely to be psychosomatic if, time and again, the child recovers miraculously every afternoon when it is too late to go to school or does not get it on weekend mornings.

The traditional diagnosis of school phobia is that the child fears separation from the mother. Family therapists would wonder if it is not the mother who is afraid of the child leaving her, and the child, sensing this, decides not to go. And family therapists would question why the mother has formed such a dependent, needy bond with the child—could there be something wrong in her marriage that has pushed her toward this coalition? Or has there been a recent stress that the entire family is experiencing so that being away from the family causes appropriate or undue worry?

This type of separation anxiety peaks at the major periods of transition in the child's education—beginning school, starting junior high and high school, and, in some cases, even when the child grows up and goes away to college. Generally, the older the child, the more serious the problem.

Fear of death, which may begin during these years, is also a manifestation of separation anxiety. Children do not usually understand death—they think it is reversible or under one's control—but they recognize it as separation and are afraid it will take their parents away, especially when they begin to see that their parents are not all-powerful. (For the child's conceptions of death, see p. 194 ff.) Given the dangers they see blaring from the TV, as well as the countless others they imagine, they fear for their parents' safety (and their own security).

Although school and death phobias are essentially a continuation of separation anxiety, this preschool and early school phase does see the introduction of a whole new group of fears—the specific fears.

It is during this period that children become afraid of persons or objects that threaten harm and intrusion, such as animals, insects, doctors, dentists. They may also fear natural phenomena, such as heights, storms, deep water, and the dark; and supernatural creatures, such as monsters and ghosts. Why do they suddenly begin to fear these things? Again, it is a matter of development; they can do something now they couldn't do so well in the past. They can reason, albeit imperfectly.

A three-year-old who shrieks and hollers when it is time to take a bath is not necessarily just being obstinate. He or she may be terribly afraid of the bathtub, and, in all likelihood, it is not the water in the tub that is so frightening, but the drain. What the three-year-old is able to do that a one-year-old or even a two-year-old cannot do is predict and imagine the future. But this imagination has little knowledge or understanding of the world to reign it in. The little girl who wails at the sight of the bathtub may be afraid of being sucked down the drain when the tub is emptied; as far as she can tell, water is no different from her.

She sees only cause and effect: the lever is flipped or the plug is pulled and the water vanishes down a hole, and if it can happen to the water, then it can happen to her. It may seem obvious to us that a girl, no matter how little, cannot fit down the drain. But the child of three doesn't always have a firm grasp on the concept of relative size—to her, anything is possible.

Children think in very concrete terms. A classic example of this is a story related by Selma Fraiberg in *The Magic Years,* her classic book on the child's psychological development:

When my friend David was two and a half years old, he was being prepared for a trip to Europe with his parents. He was a very bright child, talked well for his age and seemed to take in everything his parents had to say with interest and enthusiasm. The whole family would fly to Europe (David knew what an airplane was), they would see many unusual things, they would go swimming, go on trains, meet some of David's friends there. The preparation story was carried on with just the right amount of emphasis for a couple of weeks before the trip. But after a while David's parents noticed that he stopped asking questions about "Yurp" and even seemed depressed when he heard his parents talk about it. The parents tried to find out what was troubling him. He was most reluctant to talk about it. Then one day, David came out with his secret in an agonizing confession. "I can't go to Yurp!" he said, and the tears came very fast. "I don't know how to fly yet!"

Fraiberg called the first years of life the "magic years" because we are like magicians then—the world is a place of infinite possibility; growing up sometimes seems to be just a process of learning what isn't possible. This points up a big difference between the fears of a child and the fears of an adult. Part of the definition of an adult phobia is that the sufferer must acknowledge to a degree that the fear is irrational—he or she knows there really isn't anything to be afraid of. But for the child, what is feared appears very reasonable—he or she doesn't think it is irrational in the least. Indeed, although the young child has the ability to reason, the information, the data base, is somewhat suspect. A child can think things through to a conclusion, but that conclusion may well be awfully askew.

Three-year-old Rafer was recuperating from surgery in the children's wing of a hospital. One morning he was awak-

*ened by a voice asking him how he was. He looked around,
but couldn't see anyone. In fact, the voice was that of the
head nurse, who was talking to him over a speaker mounted
on the wall behind him. She asked Rafer again how he felt
that morning. Rafer again did not respond. The nurse's
voice became more insistent; she was getting worried. In a
harsh, almost angry tone, she again asked him if he was
okay. Finally Rafer yelled back, "What do you want,
wall?"*

*One young hospital administrator noted that the children's
surgical recovery room was a dour-looking place, with gray
walls and ceiling. She felt it would be better for the children if they woke up in a place that looked a little less drab
and so she had the room repainted. As an added touch, she
had the ceiling painted sky blue, with big white fluffy
clouds sailing across it. It certainly seemed like a great
idea until the first child woke up, saw the ceiling, and
trembled, thinking he had gone to heaven.*

The young child's newfound ability to reason effect from
cause, or cause from effect—no matter how skewed the reason-
ing—is something he or she latches onto vigorously and applies
across the board, in all situations. And it is something that is
viewed only from the child's own perspective. This means the
young child does not believe in accident—every effect must
have a cause. If his sister accidentally bumps into him, then,
according to his egocentric view of the world, it was intentional.
If X follows A, then A caused X. This even extends to inanimate
objects.

To the young child, everything is alive and everything has
a will. Which is why so many young children become terrified
of vacuum cleaners. They see this roaring, carnivorous beast

roaming across the carpet, devouring all in its path, with mother or father just barely keeping it under control (the presence of the parent helps, but no more than it would if they brought in a slavering Bengal tiger on a leash). He's a little misguided, both about relative size (he couldn't possibly be sucked in by the vacuum cleaner) and about the machine's nature (he's sure it's alive). The best way to deal with the vacuum cleaner terror (and, as we'll see later, this is common to all fear treatment) is to give the child a sense of power over the machine—show him the on/off switch and let him turn it off and on, so that reality can overwhelm the fantasy.

This animism, this seeing life in everything, can also cause fear and anxiety in toilet training. The child often does not like to see a bowel movement flushed away in the toilet because, as far as the child can tell, it was a part of him or her—it'd be like flushing away a hand or a foot—which is why experts often suggest that at the beginning of toilet training the flushing be done after the child leaves the bathroom.

Also very real and alive to young children as they develop the power to reason and imagine are their dreams, especially their nightmares. Until the age of two or so, children do not understand sleep and do not understand that dreams are not real, which is why, upon waking from a terrifying nightmare, they will not be comforted by the fact that they are now awake. They won't say, "It's only a dream," for as far as they know the beast of their imagination is still about to pounce.

It was once thought that a child's having an imaginary friend was a potential sign of trouble. Now we think of them as a positive sign of health. Fraiberg notes that young children, in a tough bind between following their impulses and obeying their parents, often create an imaginary friend to put the blame on. ("I didn't break the vase. Skeezix [whom no one but he can see] did it!") They also use these phantom friends as surrogates in coping with the newfound terrors that await them around every corner. It will be their friend who is afraid of vacuum cleaners, not them. ("Mom, turn off the vacuum cleaner— you're scaring Skeezix.")

Or the imaginary friend will be a personification of a conquered fear, as Fraiberg's classic example of a little girl, Jannie, and her imaginary companion, "Laughing Tiger."

> It is not a coincidence that Laughing Tiger sprang into existence at a time when Jannie was very much afraid of animals who could bite and might even eat up a little girl. . . . Now if you are very little and helpless before dangers, imaginary or real, there are not too many solutions handy, good solutions anyway. You could, for example, stay close to mommy or daddy at all times. . . . Or you could avoid going outside because of the danger of an encounter with a wild beast, or you could avoid going to sleep in order not to encounter dream animals. Any of these solutions are poor solutions because they are based on avoidance, and the child is not using his own resources to deal with his imaginary dangers.
>
> Now there is one place where you can meet a ferocious beast on your own terms and leave victorious. That place is the imagination. . . . No one could suspect the terrible ancestry of Laughing Tiger once he set eyes on this bashful and cowardly beast. . . . Teeth? This tiger doesn't bare his teeth in a savage snarl; he laughs. . . . Scare children? *He* is the one who is scared.

Children, then, are not powerless victims of fears. They do not like to be afraid any more than any of us do. They try to conquer the fear any way they can. Fraiberg's Jannie created Laughing Tiger to control her fear of animals. Little boys will stalk dragons, armed with a wooden ruler as a mighty sword, striving to vanquish this dangerous beast of the imagination. These imaginary friends and imaginary battles will usually come to an end about the time that fears of the imagination begin to end—age six or so.

For children of this age there are a great many things to be afraid of. They have new cognitive abilities that allow them to perceive danger in situations it never occurred to them to be frightened of before. This applies to fears of natural as well as supernatural things. An infant of ten months is unlikely to be afraid of a snake, because he or she doesn't know enough to be scared.

But it's not simply learning snakes can bite, needles can hurt, bees can sting, or doctors can poke that makes a child fear these things. The infant is not just ignorant about the potential for harm from one of these creatures, he or she is even ignorant of the whole idea of something causing harm. One characteristic of this stage of development is the child's preoccupation with body and sense of self.

Children this age wail at the smallest cut or scrape, not because it hurts so much, but because it has been done to them, it has violated their being. They love Band-Aids, putting them over the tiniest scrape, because it makes them feel whole again (and hides the damage).

It is for partly the same reason preschool and early school-children fear doctors and dentists—not just because of the potential for pain, but because examinations are so invasive and intrusive. Similarly, they squirm in the barber's chair. They have worked hard at creating their own sense of self and identity and they hate to have someone intrude on their space.

All these fears are developmentally limited. Once the child figures out that monsters and ghosts are not real, that thunder storms are nothing to be afraid of, that dogs can be friends rather than potential attackers and that there are worse things than having someone check your teeth, these various fears pass.

These specific fears are not *caused* by a child's normal development. Upon reaching their fourth birthday, children do not automatically begin fearing dogs, doctors, and the dark. Rather, at some point they become more open to the idea. Whether or not they develop a fear depends, as we have discussed, on their temperament, environment, and the state of health of their family system.

Some fears, especially those that occur intermittently, may be related to family rules (for example, which feelings are not allowed expression) or to family preoccupations or themes, those recurrent issues that are frequently discussed or emphasized.

Thunder is a good example of this kind of fear. I recall a seven-year-old patient whose mother sent him to sleep-away camp for two months during the summer. Harris's nine-year-old brother had complained bitterly that there was nothing to do in their suburban town during the summer, and the mother wanted to avoid this discontent in her younger son. When Harris arrived at camp, he was unprepared for the newness of everything—his bed, pillow, the people. He sensed that there was no one who would be immediately comforting if a problem arose. That night there was a rainstorm and Harris became terrified of the thunder, a fear that persisted for at least three years. Expression of anger in this family is taboo. Instead, worry is the accepted emotion. Thunder, then, could be described as an expression of anger, initiated at a moment when the child felt betrayed, but could not express his feelings according to the family's rules.

Seven-year-old Ernie, son of an Orthodox Jewish couple,

also was fearful of thunder, but for him the loud noise was an expression of God's anger. Both of Ernie's parents were Holocaust survivors, and they discussed their experiences frequently. Their preoccupation with the Holocaust generated a theme that manifested itself in Ernie's interpretation of the real meaning of thunder and his subsequent fear of it.

MIDDLE CHILDHOOD AND ADOLESCENCE

Most specific fears peak before the age of twelve or so, then disappear as they are replaced by a whole new type of fear—social anxiety. This is when children begin to fret about how they compare to their peers, how they look, how they behave, whether or not they will fail, or embarrass themselves. It is hard for anyone going through this phase to escape such anxieties.

Almost everyone gets a little apprehensive about appearing or speaking in front of a group of people, or of in any way being exposed or appearing openly vulnerable or weak. Therefore, the social phobias that can develop during this time—fear of speaking in public, fear of tests, fear of ridicule—are particularly strong and can last through the teens and into adulthood.

When school phobia appears in a person this age, it lives up to its name; it usually is a fear of school or some aspect of school, such as public speaking or tests, and is not a manifestation of separation anxiety (although it can be).

The child does not develop social fears simply because he or she is being exposed to more and extended social situations. Again, these fears are related to the stage of development, particularly the development of a conscience. When a child is very young, there is no concept of right or wrong—something either brings him pleasure or displeasure. But as the child starts to develop autonomy and a desire to do things independently, at about the approach of the first birthday, parents start to make demands.

The process of developing a conscience is a matter of the child internalizing parents' demands and rules. Around age three or four, a child may know something's wrong and yet go ahead and do it anyway, scolding himself or herself all the while. It is a struggle for control. Fraiberg's Jannie with the Laughing Tiger is a classic example of this. Jannie wanted to be good, so she dealt with her "bad" wishes and impulses by projecting them all onto her imaginary friend.

This socialization process continues for years. Ever so gradually the child is able to see things from other people's point of view, getting to the heart of morality and ethics. The conscience is not really formed until sometime between ages six and ten. The struggle to form one is not easy, and the child will often become a stern judge of right and wrong in the behavior of other people (as school officials have found out when they have allowed students to form their own tribunals to deal with infractions of school rules—the punishments they hand out are far more severe than anything the teachers would have given). During this age range, it may be more important to be fair than to be loved.

But as they judge others, so they worry about others judging them—or more to the point, they judge themselves. This development of a conscience, then, is reflected in the nature of the fears of this age—all in one way or another the fear of being judged.

These fears and anxieties continue throughout adolescence. Adolescence is a different phase developmentally, however, and so the fears have a different hue, although still social in nature. Adolescence is quite similar to the stage a child goes through in his second year—the paradoxical combination of separation anxiety and a desire for independence. As much as teen-agers want to rebel and be their own person and do what they want, they also want security and protection. For the first time they have to come to grips with real independence and their own future and what all that entails. The fears of adolescence remain social in nature for the most part—embarrassment, failure, ridicule, tests, public speaking—but they are colored by a general anxiety over the future.

What to Do

At the outset, parents should ask whether or not anything *should* be done. Certainly if one of these normal fears associated with the child's development is grossly disrupting a child's life or the family's life, something should be done about it.

But how about the less severe fears? What if a child becomes terribly afraid of electrical storms, or heights, or injections, but not to the point that it's disrupting the family? Should anything be done about them?

As mentioned earlier, a study found that about 90 percent of all children at some point develop a specific fear severe enough to be termed a problem. It was also noted, however, that a large majority of these children outgrew these fears, which usually lasted no longer than a couple of years. Fears usually disappear because they are developmental in nature; once the stage of development is past and the child learns that she cannot fit down a bathtub drain, that animals are more afraid of him than he is of them, the fears no longer have a reason for being. Nevertheless, they can persist.

Fears persist, grow stronger, and get worse for basically

TABLE 2
The Fears of Childhood

AGE	FEAR OR ANXIETY
0–6 months	Loss of support, loud noises, bright lights
7–12 months	Strangers; sudden, unexpected, and looming objects; heights
1 year	Separation from parent, toilet, injury, strangers
2 years	Separation from parent, noises, animals, the dark, large objects or machines, change in personal environment, strange peers
3–4 years	Separation from parent, animals, the dark, noises
5 years	Animals, "bad" people, the dark, bodily harm, separation from parent
6 years	Supernatural beings (monsters, ghosts), bodily injuries, storms, the dark, sleeping or staying alone, separation from parent
7–8 years	Supernatural beings, the dark, things seen on TV or in movies (news reports of threats), staying alone, bodily injury
9–12 years	Tests and examinations in school, school performance, bodily injury, physical appearance, storms, death, the dark
Teens	Social performance, sexuality

SOURCE: Modified and reproduced from *Treating Children's Fears and Phobias: A Behavioral Approach,* by R. Morris and T. Kratochwill, copyright © 1983 Pergamon Press.

the same reasons someone develops a fear in the first place—a combination of temperament, learning, and environment, and a predisposing family system. Perhaps a child has a fear of bees. This fear would likely go away in time, if the child's temperament is not strongly fearful, if a distortion or a cognitive misunderstanding is not perpetuated, if the fear is not reinforced over time, and if that fear is not being used unknowingly for some systemic purpose by the family under acute or chronic stress. It can be reinforced by experience (the child gets stung again), by a parent or friend who is also afraid of bees, by what he or she reads in a book or sees on TV, by nightmares, and, of course, by the family system.

A fear can also be reinforced by what is called "secondary gain." This is especially noteworthy among children with school phobia, who, as a secondary gain, get to stay home. In the case of a fear of bees, the secondary gain would probably be simply the extra attention from the rest of the family that the fear brings the child—he or she becomes special for having it, or if a parent shares the fear, the child gains an equality with that parent. This suggests again how a child's fear can be used by the family system.

Development of a fear also may be independent of the family system—it wasn't because of his parents' fighting that little Tommy feared bees, but because he sat on a hornets' nest. Although the system is unlikely to "cause" the fear, it might have predisposed the child toward it. Perhaps the anxiety of being caught up in a triangle with his warring parents created a general level of anxiety that made Tommy more prone to developing a long-lasting, specific fear—in this case, after he was stung, of bees. Or the incident became associated in the minds of Tommy and everyone else in the family with a major life-change stress (Tommy was stung on the day of his grandfather's funeral). Or Tommy overheard someone telling of an acquaintance who died from a bee sting—and no one is aware of this association.

Tommy's fear of bees might be perpetuated by the family because it serves a purpose. Perhaps attending to the fearful child brings the parents together, or perhaps the fear is shared with one parent and is used as the basis for a coalition between child and parent, excluding the other spouse. Or taking care of Tommy's fear offers a distraction and solace in the face of the loss in the older generation. In one of these ways or another, an escalating situation develops an equilibrium through some focus on the child's fear.

What should parents do? First, there are a few simple "Don'ts" they should try observing:

- DON'T force the child into contact with the feared thing, because this can aggravate the fear and make it worse.
- DON'T ridicule, shame, scold, or punish the child for a fear, for though being afraid of the dark may seem absurd to an adult, it is a very real cause for panic to the child.
- DON'T overprotect the child or focus too much on the fear, since this can aid avoidance of the thing feared, as well as raise the problem of secondary gain and triangles with parents.

The best way to deal with these normal, developmental childhood fears is to try to keep them under control from the beginning—offering wherever possible age-appropriate explanation and correction. A very crucial activity for children is play. Setting up scenarios with toys, assuming roles, etc., facilitates mastery over the feared objects or situations.

Preventing Childhood Fears

In *The Magic Years* Selma Fraiberg related a modern fable of Frankie, "the very model of a modern, scientifically reared child," whose parents set out to raise him free of fears and anxiety.

> The probable sources of fear were located and systematically decontaminated in the program devised by Frankie's parents. Nursery rhymes and fairy tales were edited and revised; mice and their tails were never parted and ogres dined on Cheerios instead of human flesh. Witches and evil-doers practiced harmless forms of sorcery and were easily reformed by a light sentence or a mild rebuke. . . . With all these precautions Frankie's parents found it difficult to explain why Frankie should have any fears. But he did.
>
> At the age of two when many children are afraid of disappearing down the bath-tub drain, Frankie (quite independently and without the influence of wayward companions) developed a fear of going down the bath-tub drain.
>
> At an age when other children waken from bad dreams, Frankie also wakened from bad dreams. Incomprehensibly (for you know how ogres were reformed in Frankie's nursery) Frankie was pursued in his bad dreams by a giant who would eat him up!

The simple fact is, Frankie's parents were attempting the impossible—you cannot prevent your child from developing fears. As closely as you monitor your child's reading and TV viewing and even what is said in the sandbox, it is still likely that your child will fear some creature of the imagination at some point, even if it is as amorphous as "the dark."

It is not even in a child's best interest to try to prevent all your child's fears. You want your child to be afraid of getting burnt by fire, of climbing out the window, of falling into the swimming pool when you are not there. What you *don't* want of course, is for your child to be afraid of things that should not normally elicit fear; nor do you want your child to be so afraid of something that can be approached safely, with caution (for example, fire or crossing the street) that it disrupts normal life and development.

The trouble is, you probably cannot prevent all problem fears. If little Mavis is playing in the sandbox when she gets stung by a bee, she might well associate sandboxes with the bee sting and, for a time, may avoid sandboxes at all costs. This is an unnecessary, irrational (although understandable) fear—but whoever said any child is completely rational? We do not have much control over what associations children make with events (nor, for that matter, what associations we make at times), or what conclusions they may reach from what they see or hear. Most problem fears seem to spring up from nowhere; you will be baffled by their source and not know what you could have done to have prevented them. Indeed, there probably was not much that you *could* have done.

This does not mean that no preventive effort is warranted. The key to doing so with any degree of success is *communication*—both talking and listening and encouraging play with appropriate toys and materials.

Remember: something you might not find at all frightening can be terrifying to a child. You have to try to see things from your child's point of view. Of course, you need not walk around your house on your knees, but you should use your imagination:

Imagine you're living out an episode of "The Twilight Zone." You're flying south for a little sun one February, but when you get off the plane at the airport in St. Wherever, it's as if you've landed on a different planet. The locals are all seventeen feet tall and they speak a language, based on English it seems, but you only catch bits of it. They shepherd you around and feed you, and treat you well, but you are totally at a loss to understand their customs. You will reach for something that looks perfectly harmless, and they will swat your hand. Then, to totally confuse you, they will drag out a huge roaring beast that scares the living daylights out of you, and they will laugh and tell you it's nothing to be afraid of.

The trick is to realize that what you say and what your child hears may be two different things. This is why we advise taking special care when explaining such things as death to a child. If you say that it is just like going to sleep, then the child may fear going to sleep. You have to be attuned to children's *concrete* line of logic and how they can come to very strange conclusions from what they see.

Similarly, you should be aware of what children are likely to be afraid of. Consoling a nervous youngster who's off to see the dentist for the first time by saying, "It won't hurt," may produce wails of terror. *It never occurred to him that it was going to hurt!* What he feared was the uncomfortable feeling of the dentist's poking and probing. Do not assume what it is your child is afraid of—*ask!*

Guarding every word you say to prevent a child from becoming frightened is, of course, just as impossible a task as making sure that everything he or she comes in contact with will not be scary. Nevertheless, being in tune with how your child thinks may help you choose your words in such a way that he or she does not suddenly start screaming at the idea of going outside in the summertime because the "skeeters" will "eat you alive." Work at it. It may not seem possible at first, but you can get in sync with how your child thinks. And when you reassure your child, try to make sure you are not really reassuring yourself; try not to superimpose your fears onto your child.

Although you cannot prevent fears from developing, or even from becoming problems every now and then, you can strive to prevent these fears from becoming such severe problems that they dominate your child and your entire family.

To do that, return to the model of the family that works well. In such a family, communications are open, the system is flexible, and the outlook positive. It is less likely that in this family setting a fear will become a severe problem, simply because the family system does not have any need or reason to allow it to become a problem.

Of course, no family is such a perfect, healthy, functioning family unit, but with open and unrestricted communication, it is unlikely that a fear will become truly problematic. As a first step, determine the source of your child's fear.

WHAT DOES YOUR CHILD FEAR?

Using the techniques of active listening outlined in the previous chapter, you should be able to detect the source of your child's fear. By providing an atmosphere of acceptance, so that the child feels nothing said will be judged or ridiculed, he or she will be free to reveal the source of fears. But suppose your communications are not so open; what makes you even suspect that your child may be fearful?

Not all fears are openly expressed by fleeing from an object or situation in tears. Indeed, children—little boys (still) in particular—may do their best to hide their fears as much as possible because they are afraid of appearing weak or foolish. Nevertheless, there are certain nonverbal clues that you should look for:

1. *Change in activity level and concentration.* Fear and apprehension may make a child either sluggish and withdrawn or almost hyperactive. Paradoxically, although a characteristic of anxiety is extreme vigilance, this intense observation of surroundings may shorten a child's attention span and affect the ability to concentrate.

2. *Appetite drop or surge.* We all know that a "nervous stomach" or "butterflies" will make us feel less like eating. But a child may also focus on eating as a distraction from a fear.

3. *A change in the amount the child talks.* Again, it may be either a decrease, as the child withdraws because of fearfulness, or it may be an increase in an attempt to ignore the fear.

4. *Regression.* This is especially common in the area of toilet training—the child may begin bed-wetting again after a long period of staying dry at night. Regression may also occur in social and intellectual competence.

5. *Sleep disturbances.* These may be as simple as occasional insomnia or as severe as nightmares and night terrors (which differ from nightmares, since they occur in deep sleep rather than during the dream period—the child screams or talks loudly in fear, can-

not be awakened, and eventually goes back to sleep
and does not remember the occurrence).
6. *A change in physical movement.* When a child's mind
is fogged with anxiety, he or she may not concentrate
on physical movement (which requires varying degrees of concentration depending on maturity) and
motions may lose grace, become erratic and clumsy.
7. *Obsessions and compulsions.* The child may become
obsessed with a morbid thought or idea, such as the
death of parents or him or herself. The child also may
become compulsive about cleanliness or about some
ritualized superstition (having to touch each stuffed
animal before going to sleep).
8. *Faceless panic.* The child shows all the signs of fear—
trembling, sweating, fidgeting, crying—even though
there is nothing to be afraid of (at least from the adult
point of view).
9. *Avoidance.* This may be manifested against school,
elevators, dogs, or certain rooms in the house.
10. *Psychosomatic complaints.* The child may have headaches, stomachaches, or similar ailments that do not
seem to have any physical cause.

Of course, any and all of these indications could be rooted
in something other than a fear. A four-year-old boy wanted the
light on at night. The family tried everything to address a fear
of the dark until they found that the child had a severe visual
disturbance. "If only someone gave me a chance to talk," he
said. A reappearance of bed-wetting may be caused by a minor
urinary tract infection. A change in activity level may be caused
by a low-grade fever or a change in exercise. Appetite changes
occur all the time throughout childhood. Thus, if any of these

indications occurs, *especially when it comes to psychosomatic complaints, the child must be given a thorough physical examination to rule out organic causes.*

When you suspect a problematic fear, the obvious task is to determine its source. Attentive listening is vital, since it is best to have the child identify his or her fear. Very young children may need some prompting in expressing themselves. And remember one of the crucial requirements to good communications—be sure your child really does have your undivided attention and that you have the time to listen.

In many instances, just the fact of telling you what is frightening them may make them feel a lot better. This is especially true with older children, who may use the chance to talk about their fear as an opportunity to boost their confidence and talk themselves out of being scared. If that happens, great. If not, don't be surprised. The reason something becomes a problematic fear is that it is not easily talked out of. Sometimes observing the child's play or even joining, following the child's lead, will provide valuable clues.

The process of identifying the source of a fear is not the time to try to "cure" the child of it. Trying to "reason" a child out of a fear is likely to be futile. Try telling someone who is afraid of flying that they're being foolish because air travel is safer than driving in a car; he or she is likely to nod in agreement and yet still refuse to get on the plane.

Even if the child's fear is based on a simple erroneous conclusion, do not try to correct it all at once. The little girl who is afraid of being sucked down the drain will not suddenly slap her forehead and say, "Of course, how silly of me," when you tell her that such a big girl could not possibly fit down such a small drain. The pace at which you proceed must be dictated by the child.

Not all resistances are fears. Take the example of four-year-old Cliff, who had a collection of pets—a parakeet, hamster, rabbit, cat, and dog. One night, tired from a busy day of play, he went to bed without eating, content to settle down with his cat and dog on either side of him. For the next few evenings, he refused to eat his meat, insisting he could not consume dead birds and animals. Some years later, in concert with friends at school, he became a vegetarian and refused to eat the school lunches. His parents' concern brought them to a child psychiatrist. The evaluation indicated no psychiatric problems. He had simply, with appropriate support of friends and regard for animals, chosen to be a vegetarian.

Fertile Ground for Fear

We have seen in this chapter that the *nature* of a childhood fear is often determined by the child's stage of development, and that the *persistence* of the fear can be the result of negative reinforcement and a family system that supports and sustains the fear to satisfy its needs. Fears are *caused* by experience and learning or, in general, environment probably supported, in many, by some inborn predisposition. As we will see in the next two chapters, a fertile ground for fear is the environment under stress.

6 Fears Related to Family Stresses

Stress is life and life is stress—you can't have one without the other. For most people, stress has a strong negative connotation, and yet stress itself is not necessarily negative. There are many types of stress, both physical and emotional. A disease or injury obviously entails stress, as does losing a job or a loved one. But happy, positive events—a marriage, arrival of a baby, losing twenty pounds—also produce stress. The way we cope with these different stresses determine whether their effects will be good or bad.

Liken your resources for coping with stress to what happens to your muscles during weight training. Picture your muscles as your coping skills and the bar of free weights as stress. Stressing your muscles makes them stronger and bigger. During vigorous exercise, small tears are made in the muscle, and when they heal, there is more muscle mass. If you keep on testing (stressing) and pushing your muscles, you will grow stronger and be able to lift heavier and heavier weights; weights that seemed heavy, will seem light, and eventually you will be able to lift weights you previously thought impossible. (Of course the analogy does not entirely hold. Although there is a way to lift and there are ways to better grow from stress, we don't say that more stress is better.)

In the same way, stress can make you stronger by straining and stretching and enriching your coping resources. Some people, however, try to deal with stress by avoiding it. But we cannot walk away from stress.

No matter how hard we try, we cannot stay ahead of stress for long, because stress has a tendency to multiply. As with the weight lifter, it's as though more weight is added to the bar every few weeks. In real life, new stresses emerge at unpredictable intervals. Like the weight lifter, we will not be prepared to shoulder the added stress if we have not mastered what we are already carrying.

What happens if our weight lifter, in mid-lift, suddenly finds that a pair of fifty-pound weights have been slipped onto either end of the bar? Suddenly the bar is too heavy to lift, no matter how well conditioned he or she may be.

Smart weight lifters never lift without spotters standing by who can help if they are needed. Similarly, people who have a social network and support system they can turn to when the demands are too much to handle on their own deal well with stress. Families with support systems won't find all life changes so stressful.

Unlike weight lifting, however, new stresses are not necessarily added incrementally; for example, if one demand or stress equals five pounds, the next one added on will not necessarily be another five or ten pounds—it may be equivalent to another twenty pounds, or four times the initial load. This is why learning effective coping from the beginning is so important—most stress does not go away, it simply gets worse.

The Family and Stress

The family is our most important, most ready, and most willing ally against stress. The family provides the essential information, energy, and resources to cope with stress. Ironically, for individual family members, although the family can be a stress *reducer*, it can also be a stress *inducer* and *multiplier*—for not only can the individual bring problems to the family for help, he or she is also called upon to share the problems of other family members.

This is why the family context is so important when looking at stress. When one person suffers from a catastrophe, the stress is felt throughout the family. In short, when one member suffers, the whole group suffers. Studies have documented this sharing of stress throughout the family. Salvador Minuchin, the family therapy pioneer, in his landmark study on physiological indicators of stress, found that children who watched their parents fighting would demonstrate increases in physiological stress indicators at least equal to that of their parents.

We have looked at the many differences between the hypothetical healthy family and the unhealthy one and found that one might not be able to tell the two apart if it were not for stress. When life is on an even keel, the two families may appear exactly the same. It may not matter that one family has rigid role definitions, does not have open channels of communication, or allows some boundaries to blur; as long as there is no major stress, everything will be more or less okay. It is when this family becomes overly stressed that things go awry and such characteristics as rigidity, enmeshment, unhealthy triangles, and lack of open communication become liabilities.

If we look at unhealthy family systems as the means by which problematic childhood fears are perpetuated, then we should look a little further, to the stress that disrupted the family in the first place so that its distress became manifested in an unmanageable childhood fear.

There are several ways of looking at the stresses that can affect a family. Does the stress originate within the family or does it come from outside? Is it a normal part of the transitions a family makes through life? Is it catastrophic, unpredictable, and sudden, providing no opportunity for preparation? Are stresses multiple or single? Chronic or acute? In this chapter, the stress that originates within the family, both expected and unexpected, will be discussed (see Table 3).

Stress and Childhood Development

Just as there are specific fears associated with the various stages of childhood development, so there are stresses that are part of the process of growing older. All new and novel experiences must be accommodated and integrated. Complex experiences—at early ages—must be understood by an as yet limited capacity. Separation anxiety is a major source of stress, for it characterizes the developmental stage in which the child is, on the one hand, afraid of being separated from the parents or primary caretaker, but on the other, is forging early independence, voyaging forth into the world. The child is caught between two strong desires—to be protected and to go his or her own way. This developmental struggle is very stressful to the youngster, and it will last for a couple of years, from a little after the first birthday up to the third.

During this period, and for many years to come, the youngster attempts to gain control over emotions and impulses. This is one of the major developmental tasks of the child—to behave according to the parents' teachings, without constantly being told what to do. This battle for self-control is not easily

TABLE 3
The Social Readjustment Rating Scale

LIFE EVENT	MEAN VALUE	LIFE EVENT	MEAN VALUE
1. Death of a spouse	100	22. Change in responsibilities at work	29
2. Divorce	73		
3. Marital separation	65		
4. Jail term	63	23. Son or daughter leaving home	29
5. Death of close family member	63	24. Trouble with in-laws	29
6. Personal injury or illness	53	25. Outstanding personal achievement	28
7. Marriage	50	26. Spouse begins or stops work	26
8. Fired at work	47		
9. Marital reconciliation	45	27. Beginning or ending school	26
10. Retirement	45		
11. Change in health of family member	44	28. Change in living conditions	25
12. Pregnancy	40	29. Revision of personal habits	24
13. Sex difficulties	39		
14. Gain of new family member	39	30. Trouble with boss	23
15. Business readjustment	39	31. Change in work hours or conditions	20
16. Change in financial status	38	32. Change in residence	20
		33. Change in schools	20
17. Death of close friend	37	34. Change in recreation	19
18. Change to different line of work	36	35. Change in church activities	19
19. Change in number of arguments with spouse	35	36. Change in social activities	18
20. Mortgage or loan for a major purpose (home, etc.)	31	37. Mortgage or loan for a lesser purpose (car, TV, etc.)	17
21. Foreclosure of mortgage or loan	30	38. Change in sleeping habits	17

LIFE EVENT	MEAN VALUE
39. Change in number of family get-togethers	16
40. Change in eating habits	15
41. Vacation	13
42. Christmas	12
43. Minor violations of the law	11

PREVENTIVE MEASURES

The following suggestions are for using the Social Readjustment Rating Scale for the maintenance of your health and prevention of illness:

1. Become familiar with the life events and the amount of change they require.
2. Put the scale where you and the family can see it easily several times a day.
3. With practice you can recognize when a life event happens.
4. Think about the meaning of the event for you and try to identify some of the feelings you experience.
5. Think about the different ways you might best adjust to the event.
6. Take your time in arriving at decisions.
7. If possible, anticipate life changes and plan for them well in advance.
8. Pace yourself. It can be done even if you are in a hurry.
9. Look at the accomplishment of a task as a part of daily living and avoid looking at such an achievement as a "stopping point" or a "time for letting down."

Adapted from T. H. Holmes and R. H. Rahe. "The Social Readjustment Scale," *Journal of Psychosomatic Research*, Vol. II, 1967, 213–18. © 1967, Pergamon Press, Inc. Reprinted with permission.

won. Eventually, after the child reaches the age of six or seven, the struggle goes beyond self-control to the forging of conscience, still another stressful task.

At school, the child is confronted with several hardy stresses, chief of which are the need to hone social skills so as to be popular and accepted, the challenges of becoming academically and physically competent and the task of moving from a small family system to sharing one or two parental figures (teachers) with many more children.

The birth of a sibling is a major stress at any time, but particularly when the child is young. There is the almost inevitable sibling rivalry, since the older child cannot help but feel that his or her special place in the family has been usurped and envies the attention given the newcomer. The child will also be affected by the parents' stress as they cope with the new arrival.

Children, like adults, can either cope well with the stress—meeting its demands with adequate resources, adapting to the changes it requires—or they can respond unhealthily. Someone has characterized four basic unhealthy response types as: *dependent* (clinging, passive, or demanding), *impulsive* (overactive, perhaps antisocial), *passive-aggressive* (seemingly agreeable, but uncooperative), or *repressed* (shy, withdrawn, anxious). Problematic childhood fears are most closely associated with the last type—repressed.

Just as with fears, how children respond to stress is a matter of inheritance, learning and social context. There are basic temperamental factors involved, as well as what the child learns from observing how the parents cope with stress. The child's greatest resources against stress are a sense of competence and efficacy (a resource that is also invaluable against becoming fearful) and a sense of support and backup. If the child can love and play well, feel good about his or herself, and has a strong feeling of conscious self-control over his or her actions, stress will most likely not be an overwhelming problem.

Unlike adults, children have a very limited support system outside the family to turn to in times of stress. Those children who cope best, however, are the ones who use what they have, whether it is an adult relative, an adult at school, or a trusted sibling or peer. Trust of peers and siblings is very important, and perhaps the best way to gain it is for the child to earn it, by trying to help friends and siblings when they need it. This helps the child forge a support system and, by helping others deal with stress, gives a greater sense of mastery, a feeling that he or she could handle the stress if need be.

Stress Caused by Family Development

We all recognize that change does not cease upon reaching adulthood—every life stage entails change and further development.

The noted psychiatrist Erik Erikson divided the human life cycle into eight stages of development: infancy, childhood, play age, school age, adolescence, young adulthood, maturity, and old age. To Erikson, each of these stages is like a rung on a ladder, but with each one very far apart so that you cannot skip a rung in your effort to reach the top. And to reach the next rung you have to resolve the conflicts presented by the stage you're in.

To Erikson, each conflict can be simplified to an "A-versus-B" situation, and each conflict can have either a positive resolution or its antithesis. In infancy, the conflict is between trust and mistrust—will the child learn that the parents can be counted on for love and care?—and the resolution, if all goes well, is *hope.* When of school age, the child will struggle with industry versus inferiority and will, one hopes, come out of it with a sense of competence. In maturity, the person is torn between generativity (rearing children, giving back to society) and self-absorption, and if it resolves correctly, the person gains a sense of caring. Seen together, the eight stages, conflicts, and resolutions form a steady progression, as outlined in Table 4.

According to Erikson, these stages are by no means achieved automatically. The conflict in each one is a crisis that could go either way. If the conflict is not resolved correctly—if the child comes out of infancy with little sense of trust, or out of school age with little sense of competence—then the next stage is in doubt. The conflict may be resolved to a degree and the subsequent stages progress normally, but there would always be the lingering possibility that the earlier failure might someday undermine further progress.

What can make the family unit so complex is that at any one time, each of its individual members can be at a different stage in their lives, trying to resolve a different conflict. A family systems elaboration on Erikson recognizes complementary development in a family in different generations simultane-

TABLE 4

STAGE	CONFLICT	RESOLUTION
Infancy	Trust vs. mistrust	**Hope**
Early childhood	Autonomy vs. shame, doubt	**Will**
Play age	Initiative vs. guilt	**Purpose**
School age	Industry vs. inferiority	**Competence**
Adolescence	Identity vs. identity confusion	**Fidelity**
Young adulthood	Intimacy vs. isolation	**Love**
Maturity	Generativity vs. self-absorption	**Care**
Old age	Integrity vs. despair, disgust	**Wisdom**

ously. So, following Erikson (not everyone agrees with his exact terms, but many concur with his concept of different tasks for different ages in an inevitable progression), while the rebellious teen-age son is trying to forge his own identity, his father might be struggling to find caring and the grandparent, wisdom.

Depending on the stages, and depending on how the resolution of conflict is proceeding, these various struggles can either come into conflict or work together. This process is, appropriately enough, called "cogwheeling," for like gear wheels, the various stages can grind and clash if they are out of sync, or mesh together if in sync.

There are also differences in development stages according to gender, following what we think of as traditional male and female roles. Society has changed a great deal in terms of male-female role flexibility over the past several decades. Nevertheless, even the most egalitarian of couples may find that their role sharing and exchange ends at the birth of their first child. Whether learned or inherited, the mother and father roles, divided according to sex, are very deeply ingrained, and each has its own course to run. These two separate courses have their own developmental differences, the main one obviously being who assumes responsibility for child care.

Not only are there individual development stages and gender-specific development stages, there are also whole family development stages. As noted in Chapter 2, the family must be looked at, not only in terms of its spatial dimensions—its structures and patterns of relationships—but also in terms of its time dimension. The "when" of a family is its place along its course of development. (Try, for the heck of it, to figure out your family's place as well as that of some others you may know.) In

Clinical Implications of the Family Life Cycle, David Kantor outlines the family's major developmental tasks as:

1. *Attachment:* making a commitment to another person and discovering the rules and boundaries of the relationship.
2. *Industry:* developing strategies for getting things done, inside and outside the family, without compromising individual needs.
3. *Affiliation:* extending commitments outward to extended family, institutions, organizations, and others.
4. *Inclusion:* allowing others to be brought within family boundaries to share its resources, affections, and identity. Mostly, of course, this refers to children.
5. *Centralization* (a task that overlaps with the others): consolidating the accomplishments and gains from the facing of other tasks. It may take years to elaborate already established structures for meeting new contingencies.
6. *Decentralization:* loosening boundaries to let people out. This refers especially to children leaving home. Like centralization, this may occur over many years, starting with the departure of the first member and lasting until the last member sets out on an independent path.
7. *Differentiation:* each member of the couple addressing the needs of self-actualization, individual uniqueness, and individualization without compromising what is right about the union or undoing the individual's attachment to it.

8. *Detachment:* letting go—terminating a couple arrangement (as in divorce), dissolving ties (as in a political defection or the breaking up of a commune),
approaching death, and sharing these matters within
the couple or family unit.

In the traditional view, the family's course is a linear one,
with one developmental task succeeding another. However, the
stages or tasks listed above should be seen more as a cycle than
as a straightforward progression, for there is a certain amount
of repetition. Indeed, it is more like a spiral, a concept developed by Lee Combrinck-Graham (see Fig. 6; also in *Clinical
Implications of the Family Life Cycle*) where three generations
are developing simultaneously, or an accordion, as she mentions
in another article, with the family consolidating and expanding
repeatedly.

Just as with Erikson's stages of individual development,
so, too, the family must accomplish each task or risk encountering problems. But the tasks are not easily accomplished. Stress
is associated with the transitions from stage to stage, when the
family has to alter significantly its mode of operation to succeed
at the next task. Troubles in families, whether a parent's depression or addiction, a child's behavior, *or a fear,* are often related
to these difficult *transitions.* Indeed, such symptoms are often
really symptoms of some sort of developmental impasse. We
could say that the "action" is at the transitions.

The family's development, then, is not just a combination
of the individuals' developmental courses. The family is a syner-
gistic unit, more than the sum of its parts. Although one of the
goals of the family is to help each member through his or her
own development, it is also concerned with its own interests and
development. This is no more readily apparent than when the

FIGURE 6.
The Life Cycle Spiral

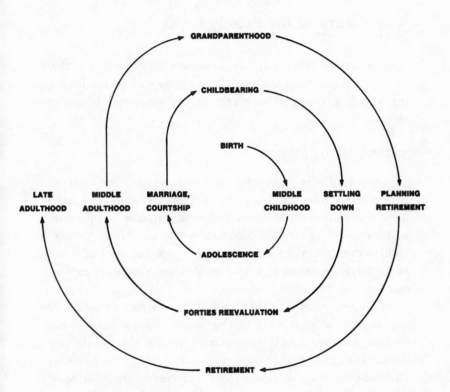

Adapted from Lee Combrink-Graham in *Clinical Implications of Family Life Cycle,* ed Howard
A. Liddle, Aspen Systems Corp., 1983.

family must group together, each member putting aside personal issues, to confront a collective task. When the task is developmental, the family may well be faced with a crisis.

The Nature of the Family Crisis

How a family copes with crisis depends primarily on three factors: the nature of the stress, the family's resources for coping with it, the way in which the family views and defines the stress.

THE CAUSE OF STRESS

The cause of stress may be an event or situation that can potentially produce a change in the family system. The family may change in size, goals, boundaries, patterns of operation, and values. The stress is not inherently negative—having a child is as much of a stress as losing a job. But part of it may be negative; for example, a baby needs almost constant care and costs money to clothe and feed.

There are two ways of classifying stress: by its characteristics and by what it does to the family. Characteristics may include whether it: (1) comes from within the family (e.g., divorce) or from without (natural disaster); (2) directly involves all family members or just some; (3) arrives suddenly or comes on gradually; (4) is severe or mild; (5) takes a long or short time to adjust to; (6) is expected or unpredictable; (7) is natural or man-made; (8) is something the family believes it can solve or is beyond its control.

Stress can also be classified by what effect it has on the

family, whether the: (1) family gains a new member; (2) family loses a member; (3) morale and unity of the family is broken (e.g., alcohol abuse, long-term illness); (4) morale and structure of the family are affected (desertion or divorce). Basically, then, stress is associated with what can, in a simplified manner, be looked at as *the comings and goings* of life.

Stress is not a single, easily identifiable "thing." It usually has many faces and almost never travels alone; all too often, one stress comes upon the heels of another, compounding the difficulty.

Take, for example, new parents. There is hardship in the financial burden, which is compounded by the difficulties of coming to terms with the abrupt transition to parenthood. There also may be the prior financial and emotional strain of the wife taking time off or even leaving her job to have the child. This may be further exacerbated by the husband taking a second job or the wife returning to work when she would rather stay home with the baby. Then, when the child actually arrives, there is the stress of the addition of a new member to the equation of family relationships and the often unbalanced "division of labor." Also, a fragile equilibrium with one's own parents may be disturbed as grandparents' role in all of this is challenged—and grandparents and parents vie for authority and appropriate roles and distance.

All of this adds up to a sort of confederacy of stress, all seemingly conspiring to arrive at just the wrong time to make everything as difficult as possible.

It has been shown that adding another stress at this time more than doubles the problems. In addition, there is reason to think that "daily hassles"—strains of everyday life—may be more predictive of subsequent illness and psychological symptoms. Such hassles might include not liking work, not enough money, too many responsibilities, concerns about weight, rising prices, crime, health of a family member.

RESOURCES

A family may possess individual, family, and social resources, all to varying degrees. *Individual* resources include financial status (usually it's the parents who have the money, but as the parents grow older, the children will often be able to contribute proportionately more), education (what does each family member know about the stress and can that knowledge be used against it?), health (both mental and physical), and personality (this can be a *very* strong resource, especially if it entails self-esteem and a sense of mastery of life's demands).

The family's chief resource is, however, the *structure of its system as a family.* All of the attributes that make for healthy, functional families—adaptability and flexibility (although not to the point of disengagement), a sharing of power, the encouragement of autonomy, a sense of team spirit and cohesion (although not to the point of being closed), and open, direct communications—apply most of all during times of stress.

Social resources include the ability to call upon a broad support system in times of need. The social network and support system provides four basic types of aid—*information* (the first and most important aid; what do others know about coping with this stress?), *emotional support* (giving people a sense of belonging), *esteem* ("cheerleading," helping people believe that they themselves have the ability to survive the stress and flourish), and *tangible support.* The latter can take many forms, depending on *economic class* and capability (the lower economic class may give time and concrete services; the middle class, money and gifts), *situation* (in an active, vital community, people will use neighbors for short-term care, such as caring for a child while a parent is hospitalized), and *cultural* background (in many cultures a large extended family is the prime social support network.

THE DEFINITION

The way a family experiences stress can also help determine whether or not a crisis erupts. While there are relatively "objective" cultural definitions of stress—sibling rivalry has such and such an effect on the family, a divorce is likely to do this and that—those matter little compared to how the family itself defines a problem. This definition reflects an element crucial to the healthy functioning of a family—attitude. Is the family generally optimistic or pessimistic, positive or negative?

A family can experience the stress as being anything from manageable to beyond control. Is the stress a potential disaster or an opportunity? This definition reflects not only the family's general overall attitude, but also its past experience with similar stresses, its values, and, of course, the nature of the stress itself (what hardships is it causing, what effects?) and its inventory of resources and whether the family considers itself up to the task.

The families that fare best are those that most often define stress as a challenge that could help them grow. Families that define the stress as a death knell are more likely to succumb to it. This harkens back to our weight lifter analogy; if you look at the weights as something that will make you stronger, rather than as something that will crush you, then indeed you have a better chance of getting stronger.

Basic Coping Strategies

Families cope with a crisis in two ways—they adjust or they adapt. Adjusting usually involves some form of reaction, often avoidance and denial, pretending that the crisis doesn't really exist.

> *When her husband died, Mrs. Santorini did not think she would survive. She sent her children to stay with her late husband's parents for a time, and she went to her sister's to get away from the house and all that reminded her of her husband.*

Adjustment like this can be good in the short term—it gives people a little breathing room, a little time to gather their resources before tackling the problem. When the whole family is being challenged to make a fundamental change in its system over the long term, however, making minor adjustments to ease the hardship is not enough. Adaptation is needed.

> *After a couple of weeks at her sister's, Mrs. Santorini returned home and brought her children back as well. She brought them all together and told them that things would not be the same as before, that she would have to get a job, that money would not be as plentiful, and that they would have to help her out. She said it wouldn't be easy, but that with the help of family and friends, they'd get through it all right, and that as hard as it may be to believe, they'd still manage to have some fun along the way.*

That is adapting. It involves a basic restructuring of the system's goals, rules, values, and patterns of operation. Adjustment is passive and reactive; adaptation is active and proactive.

For Mrs. Santorini, a new family structure or organization, with its own integrity, is created, only now recognizing the husband's permanent absence.

The basic strategies within the process of *adaptation* are for the family to turn to a *support system* for information, moral support, encouragement, aid, and expertise; to synergize and *bond together* cohesively (since the family's strength as a group is more than the sum of its individual parts); to *compromise and change* in the face of new realities.

The basic long-term goals of a family in crisis are the same as the long-term goals for a family without problems—open and direct communication, the encouragement of autonomy and self-esteem for all of its members, coherence of the unit, the establishment of a broad social support network, and the achievement of a sense of efficacy in life and a sense of control over the course its life is to take. *And patience*—it all takes time.

A good illustration involves the Bennett family, which was able to respond successfully to a child's distress and, at the same time, work through a difficult family crisis. Mrs. Bennett had suffered a miscarriage in the sixth month of pregnancy. Five-year-old Paul had been very excited about the prospect of having a new brother or sister, and the parents were devastated—this pregnancy had been particularly important to them because of Mrs. Bennett's age (she was forty-two at the time) and her difficulty in conceiving. Suddenly, the family's attitude of joyous anticipation turned to grief and a feeling of victimization.

When the miscarriage occurred, Mrs. Bennett went into the hospital for two days, leaving her husband to tell Paul what had happened. He started to cry, and that night he insisted on sleeping in bed with his father. He started asking for a funeral, just like the ones they had for some baby chicks that had died at his kindergarten. For weeks, Paul kept drawing attention to the issue, talking constantly about babies dying and asking questions about what happens to their bodies. He started having bad dreams and refused to sleep anywhere but in his parents' bed. Clearly, Paul was crying out for help and forcing his parents to take some sort of action.

Both parents had tried to deal with the miscarriage with mature understanding, but in retrospect, without discussing their feelings of anger and guilt or their misunderstandings, they had tried to put it behind them without an appropriate period of mourning and ritual to serve as an emotional closure. Paul's insistence on a funeral for the dead baby kept the issue alive. Finally, with the help of a minister and a very supportive group of friends, the Bennetts improvised a memorial service at which religious poems were recited. Rationality gave in to an expression of grief and meaningful discussion between the parents and supporting friends. Paul was involved in the service, and soon afterward, his sleeping problems and fear of being alone disappeared. Paul no longer had to be the expresser of feelings for the family; despite lingering sadness over their loss, the Bennetts were able to turn their attention to other matters and resume a normal family life.

Sources of Stress: The Marriage

The marriage is a main axis of the family system, and when something has gone wrong in the family, it's often the first place to look. But to blame the marriage is generally a mistake. When something goes wrong in the marriage, it's usually because of some sort of stress, some assault from without or within. But what causes the stress in the marriage?

Problems that occur again and again include divisive issues, such as money, sex, child rearing, and job demands. From the system's perspective, however, even those complaints may not be the whole story, but often just a representation of some deeper problem in the system. Like fears, these important areas may have a causative factor or, more likely, a convenient focus for interactive processes.

That does not mean that specific solutions for particular problems will not go a long way; specific counseling for money, sex, substance abuse can help a great deal. What it does mean, however, is if the system can be restructured, then the deeper problem beneath the troubles with money, sex, and child rearing may disappear as well.

One potential source of major trouble in a marriage involves blurred boundaries, especially the boundaries between the *spouses and their families of origin.* Blurring of this boundary may explain why young people who have not completely separated from their own homes have a much higher divorce rate than people in their late twenties and early thirties, who are generally more autonomous. Boundaries are so crucial because they are a way of determining who's "in" and who's "out," who's on the team and who's off it.

As an example, look at a TV cliché from the fifties. A young married couple, trying to make a go of it, gets into a big fight; the husband says some things he shouldn't, his wife cries and "runs home to Mama." To the TV writers of the fifties who used this device, it was the fight that sent the woman back home. From a systemic point of view, however, the husband could argue that it was the very fact that his wife had such a close bond remaining with her old family that there were any fights in the first place, and that the dispute was just the excuse she needed to run home to Mama. For her part, she may be responding to her parents' "empty nest" despair and their fears of being alone together. The issue might be reframed as an effort to maintain a status quo preventing everyone, including Mom's parents, from growing. Her husband is not sure which family she gives priority to and he feels cheated and excluded.

Of course, the wife might argue that she maintains her close connection to her family because her husband spends so much time at the office. By staying at the office and devoting so much time to his job, the husband is blurring another boundary—that between home and office—and she questions which "family" he thinks he really belongs to.

At that point the argument can really begin to take off. The husband might then argue that he is working hard to make money, and he has to because she spends so much. To which she replies that she would spend less if he spent a little more attention on her. He says he would show more interest in her if she showed a little more interest in sex. She says . . .

Now the dispute can gain fatal momentum as the accusations begin to fly. But the problem is not really about money or sex or time spent at the office—it's about all of them. Its more permanent problem-creating dimensions are about separating from one's family of origin. Even more than that, it's about each person's perceptions and evaluations of how things are and how well they jibe. Does this recently formed family have integrity or reasonable boundaries that can, more often than not, encompass only the parents as members and *not* her parents or his job?

The tendency in a marital spat, indeed in any disagreement between any two human beings, is for each person to blame the other—"It wasn't *my* fault I hit your car. You stopped too suddenly!" Like the Japanese film *Rashomon,* in which each witness of a crime has a completely different version of events, so each of us in conflict has a certain perception of who did what to whom and why, and we, more often than not, think we are in the right and the other guy is wrong.

The best way to resolve a quarrel is not to determine who is right and who is wrong, who's to blame, but rather, to try to align the differing perceptions so that there is some agreement. This means discarding ideas of right, wrong, blame, and fault winning and losing, and using the idea of systemic blame. Indeed, the idea of agreement of perceptions is not so much that both partners agree that he does this and she does that, but that they are doing something together. They must also stick to the issue at hand and not dredge up past grievances. One way to approach it: imagine an exercise in which the aim of the argument was to figure out how *both* could win. It really can be done!

A perceptual difference common to many marriages involves the question of affection. One partner often feels that he or she is more affectionate than the other and feels that when he or she makes affectionate advances, the other shies away. Unfortunately, this difference is usually expressed in an accusatorial, blame-oriented manner, as in: "He (she) rejects my affection."

The truth is, in every relationship there is usually a *pursuer* and a *distancer.* In the best cases, the roles are interchangeable, with one being the distancer for a period, then the pursuer. In many instances, however, one person fills one role almost all of the time, becomes unhappy with it after a while, and blames the other person for it (usually the pursuer feels continually rejected).

This is where aligning perceptions becomes important, for

if both partners realize that neither is to blame, and that it is just a pattern of behavior to which they both contribute, they will be able to do something about it together.

Another area of potentially crossed perceptions involves sex roles. If a couple is comfortable with the traditional roles of wife as homemaker and husband as provider—if both recognize that's what they are doing and both think it's fine—then it is fine (within their narrow "momentary" sphere). Or if they share those roles, know that is what they're doing and are happy with it, then that is fine too. Or if at some point they switch roles by explicit agreement, that too is wonderful. Trouble arises when one partner has different perceptions and expectations than the other; perhaps the husband wants a wife who has a career, whereas she wants to concentrate on parenting, or the other way around.

In the final analysis, however, the problem does not revolve around differing expectations, but around a lack of communication. It is not so much that two people may expect different things from a marriage, but that they are unwilling or unable to express their different expectations and so submerge them, only to have them fester as resentment. Opening up communications *is* probably the best coping strategy for all marital difficulties at the least it is a fruitful starting point.

The history of any marriage is marked by a series of unavoidable stresses—the comings and goings of life (ironically, all comings seem to involve goings). Each coming adds one or more members to the group, and each going subtracts one (either temporarily or permanently, or potentially, as in a serious illness). The first coming occurs with the start of the marriage itself—each spouse gains a mate, in-laws, and new friends, while, at the same time, losing, to a degree, their own family and friends. When they have a child, they gain a member, and if the wife leaves her job to stay at home, then she loses her work and colleagues.

There are many of these comings and goings throughout life, and they are stressful because the boundaries are redefined, and with each one families must again face the question: who is in and who is out? Figuratively, should we delete or add a place at the table? And if we do, think of the differences in conversation and attention to members.

The Stress of Being Parents

The marriage is the foundation and main axis of the family, but the two spouses are not just husband and wife, they are also father and mother. If the role of spouse is demanding, the role of parent can be even more so. (Usually the issue is not forgetting to be parents, but forgetting to be adults who also relate to each other apart from children.)

In our society, 95 percent of people who can have children, have them. And yet when the columnist Ann Landers asked her readers if, given the chance to do it all again, they would have children, a rather stunning 70 percent said no. Her survey was wildly unscientific—a more recent scientific survey found that roughly 90 percent would be parents again a second time around—but it did reveal a certain amount of anger, resentment, and disenchantment (as well as perhaps a self-selected dissatisfied population, i.e., readers of Ann Landers who respond).

Without a doubt, parenting makes tremendous demands upon a couple. There are the physical stresses of child rearing, which affect the mother during pregnancy and both parents afterward as they change diapers, chase after a toddler, heft a stroller, and lose a lot of sleep. The psychological stresses come under the general heading of "worrying"—parents worry about their child's health, development, behavior, as well as about the job they are doing as parents. Most parents also have to worry about money and the high costs of parenting, such as opportunities missed. And with more worrying, more time is spent parenting and less time "spousing."

In recent years, women and supportive spouses have been subjected to a new set of stresses over whether or not to continue their careers or stay home with the child. Of course, many women, especially the millions who are single heads of households, have no choice; they must work in order to pay the mortgage or rent and buy groceries. But where there is a choice, a woman is likely to face pressure from all sides, both from within and from without. She may be torn between her desires to continue her career and her urge to stay home and care for the baby. Some friends and family may encourage her to work, others may think it odd if she does not stay home. TV commercials may tell her she can "have it all," whereas on the news there may be a segment about "supermother" burnout. She may have her political vision and conviction, and that of her "significant other," challenged.

And then there are the pressures, often unspoken, from the husband. Perhaps he likes the idea of having a "career woman" as a wife or does not want to bear the financial burden of family life alone. Or he may want his wife to stay at home because he desires a traditional family (or feels pressure from family or friends to have one), or wants to be relieved of the stresses of child care and feeling of guilt if he does not contribute his share around the house or fears his jealousy is she is "out there."

Of course, part of the pressure comes from not knowing what is best for the child. So far, no grand conclusions can be drawn from the studies that have been done. Although some indicate that it is important to have a parent take care of the child in the home for the first three to four years, other studies indicate that children reared in day care are more independent and self-reliant than those raised at home. By all indications, it seems most important that both parents share a conviction about the choice, whichever way they decide, rather than there being ambivalence or disagreement. (Parental agreement about all decisions goes a long way to ward off problems expressed by children.)

When both parents work, the situation can be difficult if the sex roles of parenting are traditional, in which case the mother will have two full-time jobs—her career and her children. Studies have found that many such women work a staggering 100 or more hours per week. "I head for the kitchen and he heads for the couch and TV" is an all too common refrain. The stress is hard on the women, and not only because of added demands on their time and energy; there is also possible lingering ambivalence, as well as resentment and the feeling of absence of support.

A positive attitude is of the utmost importance in coping with the stress of both parents working. Both spouses, but especially the woman, must agree that the choice was the right one and that it would have been far worse—financially and emotionally—for her to stay at home. Coping also requires careful planning, scheduling, and sharing of duties and responsibilities. Dual-career parents should use whatever additional income they can to buy goods and services that can ease the work load at home.

SINGLE PARENTS

> *Rhonda, age eight, was with her divorced mother, Sondra,*
> *and her mother's new boyfriend in the Smithsonian Aero-*
> *space Museum in Washington, D.C. Sondra lost track of*
> *Rhonda somewhere around the Skylab exhibit and didn't*
> *see her for an hour. She presumed Rhonda was off having*
> *her own fun in the museum. She was disabused of that*
> *notion when she heard Rhonda's name over the public*
> *address system; she was directed to the security desk to find*
> *her daughter wailing. For a year now, ever since the inci-*
> *dent, Rhonda has not let her mother out of her sight. She's*
> *always checking up on Mom, and this is starting to drive*
> *Mom crazy.*

It would seem that Rhonda is suffering from separation
anxiety, fueled by her parents' divorce and triggered by the
incident in the museum. But as is usually the case, Rhonda is
afraid, not only for her own security, but for her mother's as
well. The divorce was acrimonious, her mother has been in a
series of mildly destructive relationships since then, and
Rhonda sees her mother as a victim—indeed, Sondra probably
sees herself as something of a victim and has communicated this
to her daughter in one way or another—and so checks up on
her to make sure she's okay.

This is an example of inappropriate role playing—the
child parenting the parent—and it is one of the things that most
commonly goes wrong in a single-parent family after divorce.
The reason is obvious. There is a sudden vacuum left by the
departure of the other parent and a child is often sent in to take
that parent's place. ("Take care of your mom.")

Although the two-parent family is still most common, an
ever-increasing number of American families are headed by a

single parent, usually the mother, and most but not all are the result of divorce or separation. Being a single parent has its own stresses beyond the ones common to all parents, including added financial problems (including the likelihood of lower pay for similar work), lingering conflict with the estranged spouse, the need for support, and as with Rhonda and Sondra, the absence of a "sounding board" and additional problem solver, and little leeway for getting sick or just "cooling out."

Traditionally, the financial hardships have been far worse for single mothers, who, perhaps unemployed while married, are suddenly faced with the problem of earning enough to support themselves and their children. The almost inevitable downward mobility and lowered standard of living can be severe stresses, as is being thrust into a working world for which they are ill prepared. Single fathers who have child custody may have a hard time adjusting to being the child's primary caretaker, a role they might not have been prepared for. Generally, though, the transition is easier for single fathers. They usually emerge from divorce in a better financial state, and those who do gain custody usually have been planning and preparing for it.

Lingering conflict with the estranged spouse and the feeling of being alone and beleaguered supports an ongoing level of stress. And, of course, not all single-parent households are created by divorce. Many are the result of abandonment or death, situations that in themselves are stressful and only add to the difficulties of maintaining a household and rearing children alone. Single parenting by choice may not have as much of the "victimization" side effects.

Adaptation rather than adjustment is, as always, the best strategy for long-term changes. Roles need to be changed, the structure needs to be reoriented and realigned in terms of more farsighted goals. The organization is different. For example, it might make sense for a single mother to be unemployed while seeking training for a new career, rather than grabbling any job for immediate security. This may require seeking support from family, friends, and a broader social network and support system. Positive attitude is also extremely important; the single parent who sees him or herself as inundated and overburdened will not do as well as the one who can realistically say, "I'm doing just fine."

A case in point involves Sharon Gilbert, a divorced mother, and her four-year-old daughter, Ellie. The child was terrified to be in a room alone. Probing revealed that the fear started when the mother's roommate moved out, and Mrs. Gilbert was under considerable stress trying to pay the rent herself and handling all aspects of Ellie's care, as well as managing the apartment and her job as an executive secretary. She conceded that she frequently felt she could no longer cope with the multiple pressures, and Ellie's need to always be in the same room with her mother added to the stress. After Mrs. Gilbert was able to find another single-parent family with a child about Ellie's age to share the large apartment, the fear diminished significantly.

It must be emphasized that despite the potential for added stress—given less financial security, more loyalty conflicts between parents, children assuming responsibility, and a greater need to rely on peer relationships—a single-parent family can function just as "healthily" as a two-parent family and children can grow up well. No research data have shown otherwise.

STEPPARENTING

Stepparenting carries its own unique stresses. In this country, there are half a million marriages each year in which at least one of the spouses has been previously married. An added stress facing stepfamilies is one of loss, experienced by both adults and children. This is not simply the loss of a parent or spouse, but also of in-laws and friends. To make it worse, children often fear a permanent loss of the absent parent.

There is also the question of the "baggage" that is brought from the old family into the new one. The stepparent has to cope with "instant" children, the children with a new parent. Family rules and traditions will be challenged and changed, as both parent and child are confronted by new ways of doing things.

The stepparent may feel excluded from the strong bond that exists between natural parent and child and that predates his or her arrival. The child will also continue to have a strong sense of loyalty to the absent parent and may not be happy to see someone new in the parental role. In addition, the spouse with the children probably was, for a time, a single parent, and though single parenting is by no means easy, the person may well have gained satisfaction from it, a pride of accomplishment, and he or she may unconsciously resist giving it up.

For the child, there is also the culture shock of traveling back and forth between homes, from one set of rules to another (especially if one or both of the parents is trying to use the child to get back at the other partner). For the parents there may be the problems of developmental clashing if they are at different points in their life cycles—a classic example is a May-December romance where the young new wife still wants children and her older husband, who already has children, does not feel up to having any more.

These are the basic stresses when the stepfamily is formed after divorce. There are additional stresses if the family was formed after the death of a spouse—the child may resent someone taking a dead parent's place, and the stepparent may feel awkward about it as well. And the child, depending on his or her stage of development, may develop strong fears of death and abandonment, which can be particularly demanding for both parent and stepparent.

The basic coping strategies for dealing with the stresses of stepparenthood are patience and a realistic attitude, to allow *time.* A child will not instantly love his or her stepparent, and things may be strained for a while. A child must be allowed to continue to take part in old family rituals and at the same time be encouraged to join in new ones or help create them. The stepparent cannot move in and assume all parental responsibilities right away, especially not disciplinary ones.

It is also important for both parents to be courteous regarding the ex-spouse and not to show negative attitudes toward that person in front of the child; if they do, the stressful effects of conflicts and divided loyalty will continue. It is also important to view the situation in a positive light—having different homes to visit can be a rich experience for the child; positive new relationships will open up in the new family.

The stresses of being parents, whatever the configuration, affect the parents more than they do the children, and yet, if parents feel harried or overburdened by their responsibilities to their children, their offspring will soon sense this and feel to blame. This can be manifested in many ways, but the most common is in a sense of insecurity—the child wonders if he or she is really wanted. That insecurity can emerge in many ways, but among the most common will be anxiety and even specific fears, especially those directly or symbolically reflecting separation and abandonment.

There is also the possibility that the inevitable conflicts parents can get into—over work schedules, shared duties, each other's parenting skills—may simmer under the surface, and a problematic childhood fear may be used by the family as a distraction from addressing these conflicts.

The Stress of Divorce

We all have seen the startling figures: in the United States one out of every two marriages ends in divorce. Twenty years ago a divorce was something of a shock, a scandal. Now, however, as the figures attest, a divorce is a common occurrence. Some say this is a sign of the decadence of our society. Others say there have always been deeply troubled marriages, it is simply easier to get a divorce now—and that is a good thing. Others say divorce accomplishes little but disruption and pain. Who's right?

First, we must acknowledge that divorce is not a resolution or a solution, although many people think it is (and are therefore disappointed with the results). Divorce does not necessarily solve problems, because problems can continue after divorce. If parents are in conflict over a child-rearing issue before the divorce and that issue is not resolved, then it may continue even after they are living apart.

Unhealthy triangles do not disappear when a person moves across town or across the country; instead, a parent may try to maintain a coalition with a child or form a new one to outmaneuver the former spouse. Indeed, a separation often heightens the competition because each parent feels so vulnerable. Unhealthy triangles may actually increase, resulting in perpetuation of fears, anxieties, behavior problems, psychosomatic ailments, and other such symptoms.

The old notion of "staying together for the children's sake" may seem like a good idea, but in reality it often does more damage than good; in fact, highly conflicted marriages have been found to be more damaging than a divorce. Nevertheless, children of divorce invariably suffer hardships (although permanent psychological scarring is not at all inevitable)—some exceptions are those who were abused by the departed parent. Otherwise, most children would prefer that their parents stay together even if the marriage is highly conflicted and damaging. This is understandable—the marriage is their foundation, their source of security, and they do not want to see it crumble. Hope springs eternal. Children also feel a sense of shame at the disruption of their family. There may be an acute phase, leading to fears and worries.

Although obvious, it is important to remember that children see divorce differently than their parents do. Because of the typically egocentric world view of a child between the ages of three and six, despite repeated explanations that Daddy left Mommy, not the child, the youngster will still feel that Daddy is leaving because he no longer loves little Billy or Sally. Furthermore, the child assumes that he or she did something bad to lose Daddy's love. Their thoughts may lead to ways to reunite the family or to frankly Oedipal fantasies.

Between the ages of five and eight, children are a little less egocentric. Billy no longer thinks his father or mother left him. He knows that there is trouble between the parents as husband and wife, not as Mommy and Daddy—he has heard the fights—but still he assumes that he is the cause of the trouble. He also believes that the situation is reversible and that he holds the key; just as he "drove them apart," he can bring them back together. The child of this age also fears that if he does not bring them back together, the parent who left will find a new child to love or the most visibly vulnerable parent will suffer too much.

Sometime before the age of twelve or so, the child will remove himself or herself from the equation of the divorce and understand that parents have feelings (just as the child begins to understand his or her own feelings) and that they may no longer be in love. However, the universe is still rather Newtonian to a child that age—he or she believes that one specific event caused the break and that it's reversible. Adults do not necessarily gain a deeper understanding of divorce than this themselves.

Divorce is really a long-term internal crisis, usually slow in developing, and with five potential distinct phases—albeit somewhat simplistically advanced.

First there is the buildup phase, before anyone admits that anything is wrong, although family members may suspect there is. But whether expressed verbally or not, the marital discord is evident. This is the phase most often associated with the perpetuation of symptomatic behavior—the production of unhealthy triangles, a child's psychosomatic behavior (the "sick" child), behavior problems (the scapegoated "bad" child), and of course anxiety disorders and problematic fears.

The second stage is marked by the recognition that something is wrong. This is when the system is most heavily stressed, for it is pressured to change and restructure and yet is unable to do so. The system is in great disequilibrium, as old roles are abandoned before new ones are developed.

In the third stage, the parents actually separate. Often the separation is on again, off again, making this the period of greatest disorientation for the children. Parents often get together for repeated, temporary reconciliations because of their guilt and worry over the effect on the children. This is trouble.

Without a sense of finality, one way or the other, the family cannot go back, nor can it move on. Boundaries are also blurred in this stage—who's in the family and who's out. Legal issues can also exacerbate the situation, as divorces often proceed on an adversarial basis, and outright anger and vicious, no-holds-barred fighting can occur.

The fourth phase begins with the final legal decree dissolving the marriage and initiating the process of system reorganization. Relationships are redefined (parents remain parents but are no longer spouses) and the issue of child custody is decided. As opposed to the previous stage, where blurred boundaries cause problems, in this stage it is the reverse—it is the clarification of boundaries, especially the position of the absent parent, that causes the friction.

There are two basic options at this stage for the reorganization of the family. Custody of the children can be granted solely to one parent (with the other probably receiving visitation rights), or as is more and more the case, custody is granted to both parents. There are advantages and disadvantages to each. In the single-parent configuration, the children, weekend visits notwithstanding, essentially lose a parent, and vice versa. In a joint-custody situation, children spend an equal amount of time with each one. However, any conflict not resolved in the marriage may continue to affect children more in joint custody if their parents involve them in conflicts. Mediation may be crucial to enable some joint custody arrangements to work. The last stage of the divorce is the long-term adaptation and redefinition of the family, along either single-parent or joint-custody lines.

During the long divorce process, a child's fears can become problematic. This will often occur in the first phase, when the conflict is ignored, suppressed, or simply not fully realized.

The pressure inherent in such unexpressed conflict can be manifested in triangles, which in turn may lead to sustained fears. In this phase, the fears may be used to distract the family from the unhappy truth and thus be perpetuated, and if the family does not work to change the situation, the fears may continue to escalate. The fears will usually be one of a number of manifestations of anxiety and depression within the family and will be felt by each.

Stress from Catastrophe

So far, we have concentrated on stresses that are, for the most part, predictable (the conflict of life-cycle development), or at least not unimaginable these days (divorce). Catastrophic stresses are quite different.

A catastrophic stress is sudden and unexpected, with little anticipation or time to prepare. Personal experiences are usually not relevant, and few sources of guidance or experience from others are immediately applicable. More time is spent in the "crisis" stage with catastrophic stress; there is a greater sense of helplessness, disruption, and destruction, there are more related emotional and medical problems, and there is a very real sense of danger.

Stress, however, is stress, with catastrophic stress at the extreme end of the continuum. Like normative stress, how the family reacts to it depends on its resources, how it experiences the cause of the stress and the nature of the stress itself. The coping strategies are also basically the same as for normative stress—there must be a clear identification of the cause of stress and an acceptance rather than a denial of it; it should be seen as the family's rather than as an individual's problem; coping should be solution oriented rather than blame oriented; there should be a high tolerance for differences between the family members; there should be commitment and affection, open communication, family cohesion in the face of the common adversity, flexible rather than rigid roles; and the family's social network and support system resources, which, as always, are more than family and friends, should be used. Above all, there should be perseverance, since families may have an initial period of competence, then fall apart, unable to keep up the fight for long.

Cleave is one of those rare words in the English language that has two opposite definitions. It means both to divide with a sharp blow, and to adhere and cling. A catastrophe is a cleaving experience for a family, since it can either bring the family closer together or it can split it apart.

Many (but not all) families do survive catastrophes. Regardless of whether the catastrophe is of short duration (a sudden death) or is an extended situation (chronic illness), the family will learn to cope and adapt to its demands. The effects of a catastrophe, however, extend over a long period, and immediate coping is only one concern. More important is how quickly and how well a family recovers.

The quality of an individual's recovery can be measured by the person's self-perception after the trauma. Does he or she say or feel that the trauma is an excuse to avoid further demands ("I can't do that because of what I went through"), or is it seen as something that has strengthened him or herself ("I can do that because of what I went through")? The first is characteristic of a "victim," the second of a "survivor." This extends to the entire family—does it see itself as victim or survivor?

The connectedness of the family is very apparent when

catastrophe strikes, for although the trauma may befall only one family member, the secondary stress will affect the whole system—if a family member is chronically ill, it's not unusual for another family member to develop similar, but psychosomatic, symptoms.

This again is the paradox of the family system: being a part of it helps you cope with your own problems, but it also makes you vulnerable to the stress of the other members. When you are the one suffering the most, it provides you with crucial emotional support, encouragement, companionship, advice, and aid. When someone else is in trouble, you are not exempt from the familywide symptoms of stress, such as tension, arguments, guilt, sleeplessness, headaches, and other psychosomatic complaints.

The catastrophic stresses that we will examine in the remainder of this chapter are those that come from within the family—mental and physical illness, abandonment, and death. Those that originate outside the family (unemployment, natural disaster) will be covered in the next chapter.

The Stress of Physical and Mental Illness

The stress of physical illness on the family depends on the nature of the disease—is it chronic or temporary?—and who is afflicted.

WHEN A CHILD IS SICK

Children who suddenly become ill (pneumonia, a broken arm, tonsillitis) are primarily afraid of the pain, discomfort, and most of all, the separation from their parents if they have to go into the hospital. Although there are now programs to help hospitalized children feel more comfortable (e.g., allowing parents to stay with the child, playrooms), younger children especially view hospitalization and all that goes with it as punishment. Mostly, the distress is from a strange and frightening environment and parental anxiety.

The very young child may develop separation anxiety because of the hospitalization. If at all possible, parents should remain close by, or even spend the night in the same room if permitted (most hospitals now allow this for very young children). The preschooler may develop all sorts of fears—of doctors, needles, and disruption of personal integrity—which can only be dealt with by calm explanations and reassurance. The older child may feel separated from schoolmates, may fear falling behind and being ostracized, and may even feel ashamed. This can be eased by making sure the child maintains contact with his or her class and continues to do homework if at all possible. All children in hospitals will both miss and envy their brothers and sisters at home.

Obviously, the intensity of the parents' reaction will depend on the severity of the child's illness. No matter how minor it is, however, parents are likely to fear for the child's safety, health, and survival (no matter how much they are reassured that the child will be fine). Apprehension over potential financial and emotional hardships, as well as feelings of guilt, usually unwarranted, that they may have been able to prevent the illness, may also stir parental anxiety. Not the least is the disruption of an already overburdened work or study routing with an overwhelmingly competing and conflicting demand. Also dealing with inquiries from concerned families and friends can be overwhelming. How these reactions manifest themselves varies. If a couple has been having problems, this may restore intimacy; or the contrary may occur—blame, guilt, involvement in work, remoteness, feelings of abandonment.

A sibling's reaction to a brother's or sister's sudden illness also depends on the severity of the condition and the ages of the children. If the illness is minor, the sibling may simply feel some resentment at all the attention being paid the sick child. If it is more serious and the sick child is hospitalized, the sibling may find he or she faces extra demands at home. The child may also become sick, both to gain attention and also to express sympathy for the ill sibling. The well child will often experience a mix of jealousy, anger, sadness, and fear, as well as (like parents) guilt and responsibility (the child may fear that bad wishes he or she made about the sibling have come true). Depending on the child's age, there may be manifestations of regression (including bed-wetting, getting into fights, doing poorly at school), and the development of stomachaches, depression, and other symptoms.

It is important for parents and those close to them to remember that although only one child is sick, the repercussions of that illness are felt throughout the family, especially among the most vulnerable family members—the other children. A sibling's illness can be a source of fears for the healthy children, since it opens up a world of real danger—if it happened to their sibling it could surely happen to them. Parents should make sure that the nature of the illness and where the sibling is staying is explained to the other children as simply and clearly as possible, several times.

When the illness is chronic, the sick child may go through periods of resentment, anger, jealousy, and fear. The fears may surround death (depending on a child's stage of development and conceptions of death), which may, indeed, be the ultimate outcome. The fears may also concern the hospital, which a child may come to dread as the embodiment of his or her illness. The child may even work hard to pretend to be well to avoid going there. Alternatively, children may come to look forward to the periods of hospitalization for the comfort, care, attention, and community they bring, especially when they fraternize with children with similar ailments.

Siblings of the chronically ill child will suffer the same disruptions and fears that can occur with temporary illnesses. However, the fears can be either heightened by the ongoing chronic nature of the illness, or lessened as they become accustomed to it. Siblings may feel different and ostracized by association because of their sick brother or sister, especially when there is a fear, warranted or not, that the illness is contagious. In a guilt-ridden family, the healthy child can become the repository of fears for the entire family.

Having a chronically ill sibling can also be a potentially poignant growing experience if the child becomes closer to the parents and more united with the whole family, assumes greater responsibility, and learns, early on, the harsh lesson that life is not always fair, but people go on living.

Pressures felt by parents of a chronically ill child—financial worries, fears for the child's well-being and of the eventual outcome—can strain relations between the parents, especially if the sick child is used by either parent as a weapon or ally. Conversely, the illness can serve as a mediating factor if there is an unresolved conflict between the parents (this would, of course, become negative if the illness was being perpetuated by this use).

Parents must face the possibility of major disruptions in their normal lives. Leisure time will be lost, careers may be disrupted or hindered (especially if the family has to move to get better treatment for the child), and the parents may refrain from having more children if there is a fear that the illness is genetically transmitted.

There can be great social costs. The parents may fear, or actually experience, social ostracism. Friends and relations may stay away, either out of unfounded fear of contagion, or simply because they want to avoid the unpleasant—they don't know what to say. The parents themselves may not take the child out much, because they do not want the child embarrassed, or because they feel self-conscious themselves, or because they simply fear exposing the sick child to germs or potential injury. The experiences of parents and their own families are revived and have a major impact on how the current crisis is approached.

How parents cope with the ordeal determines how susceptible both the sick child and the other children are to developing fears. Examples of unhealthy coping would include denial of the reality of the illness, laying of blame by hostile parents, and perceiving and becoming solely identified with the idea that they are victims of something beyond their control. All these make fertile ground for childhood fears that can only exacerbate the trouble.

Functional coping with chronic childhood illness is active, aggressive, open, and social. The illness is accepted, not denied, and yet there is no sense of submission. The family seeks knowledge about the illness—they want to learn as much as they can. There is optimism, faith, and courage. The family comes together to fight the illness or, if unbeatable, to work to improve and maintain the child's quality of life as much as possible. The family is creative and resourceful. The family acknowledges its sadness by crying and protesting, but bounces back within a reasonable time.

Parents who cope well also remember to balance their care for the chronically ill child with their own needs and that of the family as a whole. They also recognize that outside help is very important for knowledge and emotional support and may seek out other parents who have gone through or are going through similar difficulties.

WHEN A PARENT IS SICK

If the illness is minor and brief, the child may exhibit only relatively minor insecurity and regression to an earlier level of behavior. If the parent requires hospital care, the child's reaction may be much more noticeable.

Before the parent is hospitalized, the child may be frightened by the sight of the parent's deteriorating health, a fear that may be exacerbated by not knowing what is going on. When faced with the unknown, children take the few clues they have and weave fantasy explanations. When the parent is hospitalized, a young child may feel abandoned. The school-age child might feel ashamed and different from classmates and might also wonder whether the parent and the family will ever be the same again. After the parent comes home, the child might continue to harbor pent-up feelings of resentment, blame, and guilt.

Unfortunately, the younger the children, the more vulnerable they are to fears and insecurities, and the more difficult it is to make them understand what is happening. Recognizing this, some hospitals will allow children to stay with or near their hospitalized parents. If that's not possible, it's important that children see (or at least hear if they are not allowed to visit) the hospitalized parent as often as possible. It is psychological separation rather than physical separation that is most damaging.

It is better for a child to have a mother in a hospital across the country, if there is phone contact from her every day, than for the contact to be limited to a weekly visit in a hospital across town.

Basically, children need reassurance throughout the crisis. They need to know, to the best of their ability to understand, and appropriate to their development, the purpose of the hospitalization and how long it is expected to last. After the parent returns home the children need to feel that they can be of some help. Throughout the illness, a child also can benefit from and may need extra consistent contact with known people, such as a grandparent or other relative or close family friend. Carrying on play and other normal activities is important.

If the parent's illness is psychiatric—including alcoholism or any other addiction—the pressures and stresses are different. The initial phase of watching the parent deteriorate is often worse than in a physical illness. There could be violent and crazy, irrational outbursts. The child, with his or her egocentric view of the world, often shoulders the blame and tries to change his or her behavior ("Maybe if I'm quieter, maybe if I'm nicer, maybe if I'm . . .") to see if this will change the parent.

A parent's hospitalization for mental illness might even be something of a relief for the child, especially if it appears that the parent is improving. The worst phase here will be the parent's reentry into the home. The child constantly fears that it may happen again. And there might be something different about the parent—an absence of warmth, empathy, energy, or enthusiasm. A long time may be required for the family to regain its former level of security and trust if it is able to do it at all.

The fears of children with mentally ill parents are more general than specific—a possibly continual state of anxiety and uncertainty. The best coping strategies are the same as for any other illness in a family; the family members need to know the nature of the ailment and what to expect; they need to unite in the face of a common challenge; they need to maintain contact throughout the separation; they need to engage the help of friends and relatives; and they should maintain stability in other areas of their life.

Death

A death in the family can be the most powerful of all stresses. When a parent dies, the surviving spouse is initially hit hardest. A sudden death can be more devastating than one that occurs after a lingering illness. The spouse who has more warning has time to work through the stages of grief and to "settle accounts." The spouse caught by surprise will have to deal with all the grief at once. If there are other stresses—problems with children, or at work, or even the pressures of making funeral and burial arrangements—the pressure can seem intolerable.

Avoidance—keeping busy, getting out of the home, taking a trip—is ultimately an unhealthy coping strategy. So are obliteration (acting as if the person never existed) and idolization (making the dead spouse almost superhuman in memory). All of these forms of denial postpone grief, but don't take the place of it.

More functional coping involves being open to feelings of grief and being willing to accept them. There is no attempt to be overly rational, but instead there is a giving over to the open expression of loss and a very natural sense of anger. Functional coping also involves getting rid of survivor guilt—the surviving spouse must stop feeling guilty that he or she is alive or that he/she didn't do enough.

Many children experience the death of a grandparent. What may be most shocking to children is not so much the death, which is explainable by the age of the person, but the reaction of their parent, the child of the grandparent, who may grieve deeply. This can unnerve a child who, for the first time, is seeing a parent out of control.

Depending on the age of the child, coping with the death of a parent is devastating and can take two or more years. Children as young as seven months have shown grief reactions—anxiety, anger, denial—to the death of a parent. Absence and perhaps pulling back from others are central to this reaction. At that age, however, death is interpreted as a permanent absence. Indeed, for all children, much of how they respond to death depends greatly on their stage of cognitive development.

THE CHILD'S CONCEPTIONS OF DEATH

To children younger than three or so, death is simply an absence—their parent is no longer around. They may know the word *dead,* but they don't know what it means. To them, it's a way of describing something, no different than saying a lemon is "yellow." For such children, the death of a parent produces the most profound reactions if it tragically coincides with the child's first experiences of separation anxiety. If a parent dies at that time, the child is likely to go through the three phases of acute separation anxiety—protest, despair, and detachment.

Between the ages of three and five, the child's reaction to death changes from a "what" question to a "why." The child thinks dead people live on "under different circumstances." To them, it's still mostly a matter of the person just being absent. They do not have a sense of the constancy of people. They may feel angry at the person for going, or may feel responsible for their leaving. This is also the age of the budding scientist, and the child, who had an inkling that there is more to death than he or she knows, will ask questions: Where do dead people live? Can I go and bring (the dead person) back? What do they eat? Don't they get cold lying in the ground through the winter?

Between the ages of six and eight, the child's conception of death takes a concrete form and parallels his or her interest in fantasy and the supernatural. Death becomes a figure, a supernatural character like a witch or a ghost. And because death is personified, it can be thwarted. To the child this age, death only claims the old and frail, not the young and swift of foot; one woman recalls being dumbfounded at the age of six when a nurse who lived near her died, for at that age she thought nurses and doctors never died. (By the way, she became a doctor!) The child may also become fascinated by the facts of death, including burial rites and decomposition.

By the age of nine or so, children will usually begin to realize the inexorability of death; that it is not a person, and that it is not reversible. They will also slowly come to realize that inevitably, someday, they too will die.

HELPING CHILDREN COPE

Children often react with anger at the death of a loved one— anger at the person who died for allowing it to happen and for leaving, anger at doctors and nurses for not saving the person, anger at themselves for any imagined responsibility ("If only I'd been nicer") and for a feeling of helplessness. However, the child may also, for a time, react with indifference.

How children cope with the death of parent has to do, at least in part, with how the parent died. If death came at the end of a long illness, the child may feel some relief that the ordeal has ended—and then, of course, guilt at feeling relieved. If the death was sudden and unexpected, the child may be flooded with the demands of grief and may retreat. If the parent's death was a suicide, the child's feelings of guilt may well be overpowering, together, probably, with all of those around him or her. In all cases, extended family and family friends, especially those close to the child, should be around and very available.

In unhealthy coping, surviving parents, aware of how much pain the death is causing them, may try to spare the children similar pain and hide the truth. This doesn't work. The children sense the pain and in turn, to protect the surviving parents, try to hide their own pain.

Nothing should be hidden from children. They'll know something's wrong, but won't know what to do. And in the future they might always wonder what other secrets are being kept from them. It should also not be assumed that just because the child is not reacting all is well. Children can be easily distracted and may seem to be all through with their mourning long before they really are.

Children should be told as soon as possible about the death in a clear and direct manner. Fantasy explanations, such as "Your mother has gone into a very deep sleep" or "Father has gone very far away," shouldn't be used. Children take things quite literally and will expect their mother to wake up or their father to return from his trip. Religious explanations should also be avoided unless the family is consistently religious, for a child may come to blame and hate God for taking the parent away.

Children can also be helped to cope by taking part in funeral and farewell rituals, although they have to be prepared for what they will see (e.g., very expressive and painful wailing) and what will be expected of them. Familiar people must be with them at all times. They also need good models of grieving—their remaining parent and other adults—who show a full range of emotions and demonstrate that it's okay for people of all ages to feel sad and to cry when someone dies.

Children need space and time to cope with the loss of a parent. They need to be encouraged to grieve and to express their feelings. They should be listened to and their questions answered. They should be helped to understand just what has happened in their lives.

TELLING CHILDREN ABOUT DEATH

Preschool

1. Use brief and simple explanations.
2. Use concrete and familiar examples (e.g., animals, insects).
3. Note the absence of familiar life functions, such as breathing, moving.
4. Check to see if the child has understood what has been said and go over it. Repetition is appropriate for children this age.
5. Be prepared for questions that may sound rude and insensitive. The child is simply curious and confused.
6. Be prepared for it to take some time.

All Ages

1. Your child should be told immediately, either by a parent or someone close, in familiar surroundings, preferably at home.

2. There is no *right* way to tell a child. *How* it is said may be more important than *what* is said (e.g., tone of voice, closeness for hugging, warmth).

3. Children may not have a predictable response, may even seem indifferent. It's not that they are hard-hearted, but that they may need time to accept the idea.

4. Children need to talk and ask questions. Nothing they ask or say should be considered bizarre or morbid; it's all in the service of furthering their understanding.

5. In general, death and death-related topics should not be taboo in the family.

6. Express your own grief in front of children, letting them know that grieving is something people of all ages do. Be honest about how you feel—they need models. Let them know it's all right to be sad and to cry.

7. All important people should be encouraged to share their ideas and feelings, with no sense that one response is better than another, but that each is a way of coping.

8. Do not use fairy tales or stories as an explanation of death; children take things very literally.

9. Don't use religious explanations unless religion is a regular part of your family's life.

10. Make the child aware that not only old people die.

11. Make sure the child doesn't think of death as punishment.

12. Make sure the child understands that death did not result from sickness, but from a specific sickness.

13. After violent death, the child will need repeated reassurances of safety and security and should be told that this doesn't happen often and that most people act responsibly even when feeling bad or angry.

14. All facts do not have to be dealt with at once. Avoid giving too many details, unless asked for. Give small, digestible amounts of information. Other chances to talk will occur.

15. The child should be taken to the funeral, but must be prepared for what he or she will see. Taking part in this ritual helps the child understand the finality of death.

16. If the child does not want to go to the funeral, don't apply pressure. The child can stay at home and participate in a later ceremony (such as a memorial service) or visit the cemetery later if he or she wishes to.

17. Let the child's school know what has happened.

18. Seek help—from a minister, priest, rabbi, child therapist—if you feel stuck.

19. Make sure that the child does not take anyone else's place or role in the family. They are not substitutes. Preserve their ability to be a child.

20. Don't go on and on about your loss beyond the mourning period. Let the child get back into a regular life.

21. Try to preserve routines such as school, friendships, after-school situations, same housing, if at all possible.

THE DEATH OF A SIBLING

The death of a sibling may be even more traumatic to a child than the death of a parent. Children tend to think that death only claims old people, and the death of a brother or sister points to their own vulnerability and mortality. The trouble is, the death of a child is so traumatic to the parents that the surviving children are often ignored.

The children's difficulties are further compounded if their parents withdraw for fear of being hurt again. They may isolate themselves, unable to give or receive affection. For their part, the children may become angry with their parents for not protecting their sibling from death—why didn't they do something to stop it?—which heightens their own sense of vulnerability, for they have discovered that their parents are not all-powerful after all.

Parents can make the situation worse by idealizing their dead child. A surviving child may deliberately fail just to avoid the comparison. Or parents may overprotect their surviving children, who may in turn regress and remain immature, viewing themselves as helpless and the world as dangerous. Some parents may press a surviving child to take the place of the dead sibling. Others may impose a rule of silence about the child's death, in effect denying that it ever occurred—the deceased child's room may be preserved, as if to deny the loss by maintaining a shrine.

The best way for parents to avoid such detrimental coping is to make sure they are not using the surviving child as a tool in their own grief. They may also find that giving attention to their surviving children and their grief can be very therapeutic for everyone involved.

DEATH AND CHILDHOOD FEARS

Fears of death follow the progression of cognitive development—when the child thinks of death as separation, he or she fears separation; when the child thinks of it as a monster, the fear involves monsters. When children understand death's true nature, they fear it for its inexorability, mystery, and finality, just as we all do. There is no way to prevent these fears—they're part of growing up—although it may be worthwhile to try to correct a child's misconception if, for example, he or she fears going to sleep after being told death was like sleeping.

A death in the family puts the whole family under stress, and it can happen that a child's natural, normal fear may be taken up by the family and used as a distraction—the one fearful child gets the job of being scared for everyone in the family. This is not good for the child, nor for the other family members, who are distracted from their own grieving—something that everyone needs to do to cope with loss.

7 Fears Related to Outside Pressures

Stress from outside pressures is often quite different from the stress found within the family, primarily because outside pressures are often seen as being beyond the family's control. For example, a family will view the stress caused by marital discord and the stress caused by unemployment differently—marital discord is something the parents have some control over, the economy is not.

Individuals and families try to avoid helplessness at all costs—a sense of control is crucial in dealing with stress. If a family thinks it can do something other than just throw up its hands in surrender, it will have a better chance of weathering the storm. The problem with external stress is that, by its very nature, it erodes and undermines the family's sense of control over its own destiny; without the sense of control and efficacy children get from it, they can become vulnerable to fears, most frequently fears for their own or their parents' safety.

As with stress that comes from within the family, the stress that comes from without is also either normative or catastrophic, chronic or acute.

Normative, Chronic Stress

External, normative stresses are reflections of the family members' contact with the outside world. Sources of external stress range from neighborhood, to work, to school, to the country and society at large.

Stress is a question of demands and resources, or "fit"— how well do the demands fit with the resources available to satisfy them? And the demands go both ways, for just as the environment obviously makes demands on the family, the family also makes demands on its environment—it wants protection and support, to be identified as a unit and given recognition.

Environmental demands on the family are divided into levels of systems, each with its own demands. The basic level is the *microsystem*—any grouping that the individual is a part of, whether the workplace, school, neighborhood friends, or a church group. The next level up is the *mesosystem*—the sum of an individual's microsystems. Beyond that there are the *exosystem,* the larger immediate community that the family comes in contact with, such as a particular industry, a town, a school system; and the *macrosystem,* which can be looked at as society and culture.

Each person's microsystems have their own needs, rules, and expectations, and they may be contradictory. For example, a parent is expected to be cool and detached at work, but emotional and approachable at home; a child is encouraged to be aggressive in soccer practice, but cooperative with siblings. Not only do each person's microsystems conflict with each other, but, in a family, the microsystems of one person may not mesh with the microsystems of another.

This can be helped by the extent to which microsystems overlap (Mom and Dad share their friendships and parenting, the children have outside interests in common with each other, Mom and Dad share some outside interests with the children).

If there is little or no overlap, however, family members may be pulled in different directions.

There are also the demands of the exosystem to be considered. Company policy, town laws, school board membership are all subject to change, and coping with the change can be stressful. The macrosystem also makes its demands in the form of changing morality, broad economic shifts, political turmoil. These changes may affect immigrant families in particular, in which the children are torn between old world and new world customs.

WORK

Over the last three decades our society's approach to work has changed drastically. In the 1950s, roughly 70 percent of all families followed the traditional pattern of having a father who went to work and a mother who stayed at home with the children. Now only about 20 percent of families are structured this way, thanks to the sharp increase in the number of two-career and single-parent families.

Work causes stress because it demands something from people—parents—who already have a lot of demands on them. Excessive work hours, scheduling conflicts, general fatigue, and irritability all give rise to stress. And then there are society's conflicting expectations. Should mothers stay at home or go to work? If they do go to work, are they bad mothers? If they stay at home, are they incapable of holding their own in the working world? And how do these expectations conflict with one's own? Some people have unrealistically high expectations of themselves and think they should be supermen or women with a perfect family, marriage, and career. Employers also can have high expectations, demanding full attention and more than a forty-hour week. How about fathers? Should they be home during a child's early months or years? Should Father be able to take time from work to go to the child's school or take the child to the doctor?

Then there's the basic matter of time and energy—who gets what and when. One extreme is the workaholic who neglects his or her family for the sake of a career. The person may rationalize the work addiction, saying that the effort is needed to advance a career and build a future. But is that future worth the present cost of absence from the family? Of course, even people who are not workaholics encounter scheduling conflicts, especially if both parents work.

Child-care responsibilities are stressful, especially if it is necessary to enlist outside help. Parents can easily get into conflict over this choice of child rearing, and even if they agree, they will nevertheless worry: what are the possible negative effects on the children? What is the best? Can we afford it? Will my child miss me? Are these caretakers kind and attentive and do they have good judgment? Attitude is one of the most important factors here; if both parents are positive about a day-care arrangement, then by all indications the children will thrive (provided, of course, quality standards are met).

The division of household responsibilities when both parents work causes stress. Full-time housewives spend 8.1 hours a day working around the house. Working mothers spend 4.8 hours at the same chores. Fathers, however, spend an average of only 1.6 hours a day taking care of the home, regardless of whether their wives work or stay at home.

And what is the effect on the children? The child who feels

neglected and abandoned may exhibit anxieties, perhaps reflective of the "shakiness" and uncertainty of this family arrangement. If the child has a fear, it may be kept going long after it should have disappeared, both because the child wants attention and because he or she reflects the parents' own anxiety. If one parent is a workaholic, the resulting parental conflict may lead to a too strong coalition between a parent and child, which in turn may sustain or exaggerate a problematic fear.

The best way to diminish the effects of work stress on a family is to agree *explicitly* on goals so that each family member knows what to expect from everyone else and to consistently enforce the agreement, while leaving it open to reworking when necessary. Besides being loving, the family must now also be efficient and effective.

Optimally, there should be a balance between work and family. Demand should be rated according to priority. Does Dad's bowling or Mom's triathlon training take priority over spending time with the children? Openness to change and flexibility in the face of changing demands is important. Though there may be some resentment initially, it will be expressed and then dissipate.

A willingness to look outside for assistance and advice from support groups (e.g., confidantes or veterans of your problem) and an effort to change factors at work that are harming the family are also important in problem solving. Fortunately, there are signs that society is beginning to be more accommodating to family needs. Examples include the move to grant both parents parental leave, job sharing, and flextime arrangements that allow people to choose when to begin and end their workday or to restructure their work weeks into four ten-hour days instead of five eight-hour days.

RACISM

Despite all the social reforms of the past few decades, minorities in our society are still treated differently than the majority. The most prominent minority in American society, both numerically and historically, are blacks. Racism has been called a "mundane extreme environment," or climate, somewhat akin to the cold that Eskimos in the Arctic must face—a constant, all-pervasive factor that people must somehow adapt to. For example, a prominent black professional mentions the frequent, daily "miniinsults"—people moving back when he gets in line, being mistaken for a janitor in his place of business, the awareness that he could be shot if he runs for a bus in a predominantly white neighborhood, empty taxis passing him by and then picking up whites.

This climate of racism is supported and propagated, often unconsciously, in the media, at home, and in the workplace. Of course, overt racism is a powerful stress inducer (a family is denied housing because it is black; a child is ostracized at school because of race or ethnic differences). The victims feel compelled to act strong in the face of multiple insults, some of which are apparent only to them. Racism, like a constant low-grade fever, is a stress intensifier, boosting the effect of other stresses—it makes everything worse.

Later in this chapter unemployment is described as a catastrophic external stress. But for many black families in America it is almost normative. The unemployment rate among blacks is twice that of white Americans, and it's even worse among black youths. Even blacks who are employed are at a disadvantage, earning less money for comparable work. Education has always been highly prized in the black community as a "ticket out" of poverty, but because of both little familial financial support and perceived and real insensitivity and concern in the school system, lack of adequate education contributes further to the bleak employment situation.

There are many other distressing statistics—the rate of infant mortality among blacks is almost twice that of whites; half of all black families are headed by single parents. Since blacks earn less than whites, their choice of housing is limited. And blacks are less able to afford preventive medical treatment and insurance. Of course, the true depth of the problem cannot be expressed by statistics alone; the feelings of vulnerability, limited opportunity, and lack of hope perpetuate the situation.

Our purpose here is not to assess blame, but instead to note that the underlying pressure of the racial climate can exacerbate other stresses. Adding stress onto stress is not simply additive; instead, it multiplies the effect. Living in the "mundane extreme environment" of racism, such stresses as unemployment and marital strife are more likely to have a negative effect because the pervasive stress of racism can bring out the worst in a family.

One also should keep in mind that what may appear to be an obvious manifestation of attitudinal issues with social underpinnings may have a parallel family problem that needs attention. I recall the case of four-year-old James, the only black child to attend a private school far from his neighborhood in a middle-sized midwestern town. His mother, a night nurse, brought him to school every day, waited until school was out, and then took him home or to a play date, where she also waited.

James refused to eat at school or at a friend's home, although he had an excellent appetite at home. His only explanation was that he was not hungry. Although family anxiety about "making it" in an alien setting can be communicated and, in fact, make the child lose his appetite for anxiety, in this family other issues were emerging.

The marriage was troubled for several reasons; the mother was left with all the responsibility for the son and the parents constantly argued over where the son should go to school. The solution to James' immediate problem lay in his parents resolving their conflict over a division of labor within the family and also coming to grips with where James should go to school and their motivations for seeking a private school outside their own neighborhood.

Interestingly, we do not encounter specific childhood fears that can be attributed to racism, although fears may arise from other stresses. Significantly, minorities often cope with the stress of racism, either overt or covert, by closing ranks. In minority communities, there is considerable emphasis on a help-exchange network of family and friends and the broader community. Within the family there is a flexibility in roles and shared child care and informal adoptions.

Addressing the underlying cause of the stress—the racism itself—and eliminating it appear to be elements of a lifelong struggle for all of us to engage in.

RURAL LIFE

Many in America idealize rural society as the "real" America. We see it as the bucolic backbone of the nation. In reality, however, rural life, even before the current tragic farm crisis, has never been that idyllic. In fact, living in the country can be a bit like being black—a mundane, extreme environment. The stresses of city life—crime, overcrowding, pollution, high prices, the fast pace, brutal competition—are well known. Less well known are the stresses of living in the country.

When compared to urban areas, rural communities, as a group, have higher malnutrition, higher infant and maternal mortality, more unemployment and underemployment, a higher increase in divorce, and more substandard drinking water, sanitation, and housing. One in nine city dwellers fall below the poverty line; the rate is one in six for rural dwellers. And, to make matters worse, there is a continued, high level of migration of the young to the cities, which saps rural communities' strength. The situation is even worse for rural blacks.

And yet there is a paradox: people who live in the country still report a higher level of happiness and satisfaction than do city dwellers. The mystery is: why? The common perception that there is greater kin and community support in rural societies is not supported by empirical evidence. By all indications, people who live in the country probably do not cope any better with the pressures of modern living than do their city cousins. Perhaps the stress is more extended and does not have the sense of bombardment modern urban life has. It seems, however, that they have a more positive outlook—they are sure they will survive the stress—and that can go a long way to determine their feelings of happiness and satisfaction.

Catastrophe

Experience is important in coping with catastrophe. To people in the Caribbean, for example, hurricanes are not the catastrophes they would be to many of us; they know that they come along almost every year, know what to expect and know how to prepare. To the people who lived along Buffalo Creek, West Virginia, in 1972, however, the dam disaster and subsequent flood was indeed a catastrophe—it was sudden, unexpected, and they hadn't any way to cope with it.

Catastrophes within the family—illness or death—cause severe stress, but catastrophes that come from outside may be either more or less stressful. Stress can be heightened by a feeling of helplessness—not only is the cause of the stress beyond the family's control, as it is with an illness or death, but there is no apparent solution and coping seems beyond the family's scope. But the fact that the catastrophe comes from outside the family can also make it less stressful if the family bands together against it and if it teams up with other families in a similar situation.

Of all the causes of stress, external catastrophes are very likely to cause sustained childhood anxiety and fear problems. These fears may be related to a specific incident—the child becomes afraid of going outside after the family has gone through a tornado or is terrified of water after a flood—or they may just spring from the family disruption caused by such catastrophes.

Family plays a vital role in how people cope and respond to catastrophic stress. Research by psychiatrist Dr. Lenore Terr on the Chowchilla kidnapping of a busload of schoolchildren in the late 1970s has shown that although some fears and stress reactions are common among all children who experience the same trauma, many of their reactions are quite individualized, depending on the child's personal history, his or her stage of development, and, of course, what the child's family is like.

UNEMPLOYMENT

Many of us overlook unemployment when listing catastrophes, but to families suffering through joblessness, catastrophe is not too strong a term.

Unemployment statistics strongly correlate with a community's number of suicides, mental hospitalizations, and homicides. Unemployment is also related to higher total mortality and, specifically, to increased deaths from heart and kidney disease. It is related to increased anxiety and psychosomatic ailments. Lowered self-esteem, although not as easily expressed in statistics, is also common among the unemployed. Hopes and beliefs in God and country are shattered.

The effects of unemployment on the family are wide-ranging. The economic uncertainty disrupts the entire system and can lead to its deterioration. It has been associated with instability and problems in the marriage, with authority and discipline troubles, and with family violence.

Unemployment, of course, varies according to age, sex, race, and level of skill, as well as by geographic location, time, and industry. Still, when unemployment strikes, its effects are somewhat universal.

The chief and most obvious type of stress associated with unemployment is financial hardship—anything below what the family needs to live on, or an income that is at least 30 percent below what it was before. The magnitude of the hardship depends on the family's resources, eligibility for unemployment insurance, length of employment, and prior income, as well as company and union policies (some companies will maintain benefits for a year, others will give more severance to people with greater seniority) and the ability of support systems to make resources available. The financial hardship can also cause a shift in the family; the wife, if she was not already working, may have to take a job. Older children also may go to work to ease the burden. And there may be communitywide financial hardship, as is common when a major employer in an area lays off a large number of people.

Another stress is the diminished role of the main wage earner, which can pose both social and psychological problems. The effect will be particularly devastating in a family with highly traditional roles. For the unemployed father-husband, loss of work means loss of status in the eyes of his family, community, parents, and himself. It also means loss of purpose and a certain loss of identity. Work is also a social environment, and much of that is lost with the job. In some cases, when a plant has been a major employer in an area for years, its closing can seem like a death—a member of the community has passed on.

There are also the day-to-day stresses of suddenly having the main wage earner at home every day, disrupting the routine. The upheaval in roles is most destructive if the family is highly traditional and if the wife has to take a job, a shift that may make the husband feel resentful, emasculated, and powerless.

The psychological effects of unemployment—anxiety, lowered self-esteem, depression—can extend throughout the family like a contagion, most often to the children. Children quickly pick up on the parents' worry and may develop a general sense of apprehension and insecurity, shame and disenchantment, and fear that the parents can no longer provide for and protect them. The child may, with anxiety and trepidation, feel that he or she has to "take over."

A child's fears also may reflect the disruption of the marriage caused by changes in role and status. The family may use a specific fear or phobia to focus on as a distraction from the parents' conflict and all the other problems associated with unemployment, consolidating the worry into a more manageable package—the child.

There are several mediating factors that can either intensify or diminish the stress. Suddenness is key. If the job loss is routine, perceived as normal or manageable, then the effects won't be as severe. Seasonal job loss among fishermen, ski lift operators, and the like is not really catastrophic—albeit very difficult—because it happens every year, and people learn to adapt to it and plan for it. Temporary job loss—perhaps an auto plant has to retool for a new line of cars—is also grim, but not so catastrophic if the workers know they will be going back.

Advance knowledge is important. If someone knows six months ahead of time that a job is going to be terminated, he or she can prepare for it—not that that period of preparation and waiting won't also be terribly stressful or unproductive.

The degree to which the individual was responsible for the job loss is another mediating factor. It will be more stressful if the person thinks that losing the job was his or her fault; the stress will be intensified if other family members also blame the person for the job loss, especially if this person's vulnerability has been an issue before. It's hard to avoid feeling that there must have been some way one could have kept the job. No one wants to think that something is completely beyond his or her control. This blame taking and giving compounds the sense of failure, which in turn adds to the stress.

Perhaps the most important mediating factor is the family's list of resources, both financial and systemic. If the parents own their own home and have substantial savings, and if the children are older (and can contribute if necessary), the stress is reduced. On the other hand, the stress is multiplied if the family consists of young parents with small children and many debts, isolated from the extended family. The family's systemic resources include its ability to adapt, to be flexible, to be optimistic, and to band together in the face of adversity. Also important is a vital support network of family, friends, and neighbors.

Coping with unemployment is never easy, and many people feel victimized by it and become passive and clinically depressed. If at all possible, one should be active, flexible and ready to take whatever steps are necessary to ensure basic stability and reduce the family's vulnerability.

Some steps to take are: ask other family members to pitch in temporarily as earners; realign the roles in the family to allow for people doing different tasks; practice good financial management, which may include some cutting back on spending; maintain and strengthen relationships within the family and with the support systems of family and friends; and join with others in the same situation to attempt shared problem solving, support, and action. All of this is done best with the awareness and agreement of the whole family, using active parental leadership.

There are obvious costs connected with these strategies. Having other family members enter the work force creates new stresses at home, especially if the home is traditional and the unemployed father-husband resents the new situation and is unwilling to do his part around the house. And though social network support is important, if it is too strong it may anchor a family to a place it may be in their best interest to leave.

Perhaps the most important coping strategy is to define the unemployment as a challenge to be surmounted, not as a demoralizing defeat, and to look at it as an opportunity for change and a means for keeping activity, not retreat, in the forefront.

DISASTERS

Disasters are hardly new; even before Noah built his ark our ancestors faced all of the natural calamities that afflict us today. For the most part they are the cruel whims of nature, but increasingly we are called on to deal with man-made disasters as well. Wars, the tragic chemical leak at Bhopal, the Chernobyl nuclear disaster, terrorist attacks—these are but a few examples. Whether natural or man-made, all disasters have a similar profound impact on individuals, families, and whole communities. Two characteristics make disasters different from other catastrophes—they can be experienced by whole communities, and not just one family; and they are often experienced by the whole family together. An entire country may experience a disaster vicariously through the media, as was the case with the 1985 terrorist kidnapping of the TWA airliner and the January 1986 Challenger shuttle explosion.

There are roughly thirty major natural disasters each year, taking the lives of 250,000 people and costing the world's economy tens of billions of dollars. In the United States alone, disasters cost upward of $5 billion each year in prevention and in restoration costs, and take 600 lives. The major types of natural disasters are floods, hurricanes and typhoons, earthquakes, and drought. Ninety-five percent of the deaths from disasters occur in the developing nations, although the industrialized nations bear the greater economic loss.

Even though the number of natural disasters each year remains steady, the cost in money and lives has risen sharply over the past few decades. This is partly due to population increases and concentration in disaster-prone areas. Consider that in the United States over half the population lives along coastlines, susceptible to hurricanes or earthquakes.

Disasters vary in type—flood, earthquake, tornado, blizzard—and in suddenness, duration, intensity, the number of lives lost, short- and long-term hardships, and economic costs. Generally, the worst disasters are those that come suddenly at night, without much warning, hit hard, and have prolonged effects. But even disasters with advance warning can play havoc with a family, far beyond the immediate impact of the event itself. For example, if there is time to prepare—as in the case of a slowly spreading drought—the family actually may be disrupted and torn apart for longer than if the disaster comes and goes quickly. If the disaster is a persistent threat or becomes recurrent, then the community can adapt and learn to prepare. For example, people in earthquake-conscious Los Angeles know that they should stand away from windows and in a corner or doorway, the strongest places in a building, if they feel a tremor.

Some disasters may even have a positive result, especially if they bring a community together. If it survives relatively intact, the community may emerge with a sense of optimism and a feeling that it can weather almost anything.

That sense of enthusiasm and solidarity does not always last, however. Theorists have divided the response of a community to a disaster into four emotional stages. First is the heroic stage—the immediate response to the threat, when everyone bands together altruistically. Second is the "honeymoon," which lasts from one week to half a year, when the community is eager and optimistic to rebuild, buoyed by promises of aid and relief from outside. Next follows a period of disillusionment, which may last for a couple of years; when the promised aid does not appear and rebuilding does not proceed as planned, the sense of community sharing and team spirit may evaporate and be replaced by disappointment, in-fighting, and resentment.

Finally there comes reconstruction, which may take several years, when the community decides it has to take care of itself and it regroups, looking to the future with tempered optimism.

Much of how a community reacts to disasters depends on whether it is an individuated or kin-oriented community. Individuated communities are generally urban, where the connections are between friends and neighbors, and where nuclear rather than extended families predominate. Kin-oriented communities are usually rural, and the connections are usually along broad, extended family lines and not so much with outsiders. Individuated communities are usually better equipped to react to a disaster, to adapt and cope with the exigencies. But though kin communities are less flexible, less able to adjust to the disaster on the short term, they are better in reestablishing the community on a long-term basis. The most vulnerable communities are often those in developing countries, caught between burgeoning urban individuation and strong ties to kin-oriented villages.

Although disasters affect whole communities, the primary unit of response is the family, for that is how people bind together against adversity. And much of how a family responds depends not only on the severity of the disaster and the community's response, but also on how the the family defines the event, for the more the family views the adversity as a disaster, the more it will become one.

The individual, however, bears the brunt of any disaster. Unlike most other sources of stress, there is a very real risk of physical danger, even death. There is also disruption and destruction and likely considerable personal loss, increasing the sense of helplessness. The efficacy of the individual's reaction depends on basic stress-coping abilities, his or her role in countering the disaster, previous experience, and, most important, a general feeling of adequacy or inadequacy.

Many emerge with survivor guilt. Or a person may feel responsible for the outcome. (Why didn't I stay at home? Why didn't I stock canned goods? Why did I move to Los Angeles?) And there will be fears—of further destruction, of it happening again, of being unable to cope.

As always, children are the ones most vulnerable to developing these fears. Research has found that fear- and anxiety-related disturbances are the most frequent psychological problems found among children who have survived a disaster. Ranked in order of prevalence, the ten most common such psychological problems are:

1. Anxiety disorder, avoidant disorder;
2. Anxiety disorder, separation anxiety disorder;
3. Sleep-terror disorder;
4. Overanxious disorder;
5. Simple phobia;
6. Agoraphobia, without panic;
7. Post-traumatic stress disorder, acute;
8. Post-traumatic stress disorder, chronic;
9. Attention-deficit disorder with hyperactivity; and
10. Attention-deficit disorder, residual type.

The first six are anxiety and fear related. An example of avoidant disorder is when the child stays away from anything related to the disaster. A simple phobia is a specific fear of an object, situation, or activity, either directly or symbolically related to the disaster. Agoraphobia is a broad fear, usually of going outside, although it could be of anything or everything. With separation anxiety, the child is afraid of being parted from his or her parents and their protection. Overanxious disorder is akin to general anxiety disorder in adults; it is an all-pervasive sense of dread, caused by a feeling of insecurity, for now the child has seen that neither parents nor family are invulnerable. Sleep terror is the worst of the sleep disturbances common among children after a disaster. It differs from a bad dream or nightmare in that it is a sudden, unfocused, all-pervasive feeling of dread and terror.

These fears and anxiety disorders are the more long-term effects of the disaster. There also are initial short-term reactions that parents should watch for. The most common are:

1. Sleep disorders (before reaching the severity of night terror, there may be a simple fear of sleeping, an inability to sleep, disquieting dreams);
2. An exaggeration of separation anxiety;
3. Fear that the disaster will happen again;
4. Avoidance of reminders of the disaster;
5. Hyperalertness;
6. Psychosomatic illness; and
7. Regression in younger children to bed-wetting, thumb sucking, and dependence; and conduct disturbances.

These fears and distrubances should be dealt with at this point, before they progress. In general, the problem should be tackled on a family basis, especially because other family members may also experience fears, anxieties, phobias, and sleep disorders. Although a certain amount of fear and anxiety is normal after a disaster, the severity depends, to a large degree, on how well the family copes with the disaster. Second, the child must be made to feel that it is normal to have these fears and other reactions; indeed, everyone has them, to an extent. Third, attention must be paid to the child, but it should not be overattention (due to the parents' irrational sense of guilt over "failing" as parents because they did not completely protect their child from the disaster).

A disaster can be the ultimate source of stress, and it tests the resources of a family and community very quickly, distinguishing the healthy from the unhealthy, the adaptable from the unadaptable. If a family is shaky under normal levels of stress, then it can be overwhelmed easily by a disaster. Unhealthy coping can be characterized by a family's ignoring warnings and threats of an approaching disaster, not only because they hope it will go away, but because they know they will be unable to cope if and when it comes. Afterward, when this family needs to be flexible and adapt, it will be rigid and intolerant. Family members may long for their predisaster routine, but will be unable to reestablish it. With little drive to rebuild, the family is likely to give up; it will see no future and will be plagued by doubts and fears. Outside aid and help may be shunned, or, conversely, the family will rely almost entirely on aid instead of on its own resources.

The family with healthy coping abilities approaches the disaster and its aftermath differently. There are several characteristics of effective coping with a disaster:

1. Being prepared, both physically (knowing the potential dangers of the region, rehearsing escape drills) and psychologically (having a sense of efficacy and adequacy);
2. Having had previous experience with disaster;
3. Possessing basic coping resources;
4. Working together as a cohesive team;
5. Exhibiting flexibility and tolerance of change;
6. Having a history of acceptance and support between family members in other crises;

7. Exhibiting an active, rather than passive, utilization of family, friend, and community support networks;
8. Availability of a professional helping network, even if it comes from outside the disaster area.

There is one more key to functional coping with disaster, and it is perhaps the most important of all—attitude. It is not just a matter a defining the disaster either as a challenge or a defeat, but rather of the family defining itself as either survivors or victims. People may not know how they will react until a crisis happens, at which point they may find they have more reserves than they had anticipated.

WAR AND CAPTIVITY

Children brought up in war-torn areas show a remarkable ability to adapt and cope with the constant presence of terror. In a way it's similar to the mundane extreme environment of racism, except that the baseline of stress is much more severe, much more heightened, and astoundingly dislocating.

War, in terms of stress, is like a severe disaster that comes, then never goes away. The reaction to it, however, is not the same as it is in communities that have learned to live with yearly floods. War is far less predictable. No one knows when the shelling will begin again, or when another raid will come through the village. There is a constant level of uncertainty, of apprehension, of fear and anxiety.

The whole community somehow adapts to life during wartime, including the children. The children may seem to be much like children anywhere, and they may seem to treat war as normal. Nevertheless, they are deeply affected, with potential personality effects, fears and anxieties, much like those produced by disasters, only more long-lasting.

Children in the United States have been spared the experience of a war at home. They may, however, know someone who has gone to war or will in the future. Young children usually experience a great deal of separation anxiety when their fathers are off at war. When they are older and understand better what war is, they may have fears for their father's safety, as well as fears born of insecurity and the threat of not having their father's protection anymore. Now, of course, much of the public reaction to war is not as a crucible for heroism, but as a failure of a government's integrity and as a self-serving vehicle with soldiers as victims of their own government.

Captivity of a parent poses other problems, especially if the parent's fate is unknown. In such instances, the family may go through all the stages of grieving, yet not be able to resolve it. The family may stagnate because of the uncertainty and ambiguity of the situation and a seething anger at this lack of closure. If the family learns that the parent in captivity has died, there may be an initial feeling of relief at finally knowing the parent's fate; but this will soon be followed by inevitable grieving and mourning, and all that that entails for the family and its children. Children may suffer from separation anxiety and fears for their own and their parent's safety. Obviously, this is to be expected.

Counselors suggest that families with family members at risk for an extended period of time try to cope just one day at a time.

In general, the best way to cope with the stress of war is the way to cope with all catastrophe—to somehow stay optimistic and actively try to reduce stress, to connect with others in a similar situation, and, as an ultimate goal, eliminate the source of the stress. Children can cope better if adults are open with them, revealing as much as possible about what is happening. Adults must also be open about their own fears, concerns, and anger, to let children know that they are not alone in how they feel.

Throughout this book we have emphasized that fears usually persist only when they are sustained by some need of the family system. But in the case of war and captivity, which are ongoing, virtually unprecedented, and terribly threatening experiences, a mother may nurture a child's fear as a distraction from her own unceasing worry over the fate of her husband, and a child's anxiety or other symptom may realistically persist though having little to do with the family's response.

CURRENT EVENTS

One of the liabilities (or advantages) of having such extensive worldwide media capabilities is we are exposed to vicarious stress. In the past, people were only stressed by events they came into direct contact with. Now, however, with the amount of information available, there is added, vicarious stress. Reports of serial killers, airplane hijackings, suicide bombers—all these contribute to a widespread mundane extreme environment, which can, and does, have an effect on children.

Studies undertaken to measure the effect the threat of nuclear war has had on children have been inconclusive; some report it has contributed to children being fearful, others say not. Perhaps it is something children become accustomed to. Nevertheless, when, for whatever reason—the anniversary of Hiroshima, the airing of the TV movie *The Day After*—the subject gets prominent new coverage, children do become apprehensive for a time, and much of the problem is a lack of knowledge, knowledge that adults are reluctant to share with children for fear of scaring them. Indeed, as one child said, "Kids ought to be afraid of nuclear war, but they don't know what it is." Many youngsters of appropriate age sense that they lack a future because of the nuclear threat and dwell on ultimate destructive events. Some are reassured by activist efforts of families and communities to try to bring about change, as well as by factual education. Up to the age of eight, children may express fears, but also can be reassured. From about ages nine to eleven, they will ask about facts and indulge in violent fantasies, even while seeking reassurance. Beyond that age, there is a gradual desire for kids to make up their own minds from facts, feelings and ideas. It is important for parents to keep up with the writings on this.

The AIDS crisis has become as much an epidemic of fear as an epidemic of disease. Children have been made fearful about this in an unhealthy way by the debate over whether children with AIDS should be allowed to go to school with other children. Children often feel that *all* illness is contagious so that the understandable, but ill-founded, hysterical fears of parents have only made children intensely afraid of something they know very little about. Here, irrational fear can be greatly reduced by legitimate information and a parental coalition of approach.

When the space shuttle Challenger exploded in January 1986, the entire nation was traumatized. Children were particularly affected, as they all watched on TV to see the first teacher, Christa McAuliffe, fly into space. The reaction among children was almost universal. What happened? Was it real? Was it just TV? Writing to Mrs. McAuliffe's family helped some children get over their feelings of guilt and helplessness.

In general, fears may spring out of such sudden, large-scale but vicariously experienced traumas or anticipated disaster, but they usually will not last too long; the child, no matter how frightened, still does not have an immediate and ongoing attachment to the people involved. More long-term external threats, such as the specter of nuclear war or the spread of AIDS, may well produce a lower level of stress that percolates beneath the surface. Like the stress of less obvious racism, these threats may act as stress intensifiers, making other stresses seem stronger.

The stress from such external threats should be dealt with through careful reassurance and explanation—giving the facts about how AIDS is spread; explaining that the shuttle explosion was just a terrible accident and that people will find the cause so it won't happen again; explaining, as best one can, the theory of nuclear deterrence. Fears arising out of this type of stress are, like most other fears, only likely to become problems if they can connect realistically or symbolically to other issues and if the family responds to them in a way that sustains or exaggerates them, which may be a reflection of other family members' fears (if a mother is terrified of AIDS, her child's fear might be strengthened) or a reflection of some need for distraction that the family has.

TV watching provides information that, depending on the age of the child, may be like listening to a foreign language with which a person has only partial familiarity. Misunderstanding may be the rule. Moreover, parents may discuss current events in such a way as to punctuate the TV watching. For example, they may use expletive or derisive comments, and in doing so, the child may focus even more on the specifics that trouble or frighten parents and end up inheriting those fears.

The Importance of Coping

The stresses that come from outside the family are more likely to be met with ineffective coping. When problems are manifested in a marriage, a husband and wife can't escape the fact they have the power to make needed changes—it's largely a matter of whether they want to make the effort and know how or find the "key!" When there are problems in balancing the demands of work and home, however, they can blame it on the workplace and say it is beyond their control.

External stress contributes to this feeling of powerlessness because, indeed, much of it is beyond the family's immediate control—one can't stop the company from shifting its manufacturing to Korea and closing the plant in town; one can't erase racism or change the course of a tornado. It's often tempting to throw up one's hands in surrender.

But even if the original source of the stress may be beyond the family's control, the family does control its response; the first thing it should do is take up the fight rather than give up. By taking an active initiative and seizing as much control as possible, the family can do much to head off future problems, such as childhood fears.

Some childhood fears, especially those associated with disasters, are unavoidable. But fears that run beyond the length of their normal expected course, fears that become problems, are avoidable.

8 Families— Heal Thyselves?

The basic premise of this book is simple: a childhood fear is not likely to become a problem unless it is sustained or exaggerated by the family. Indeed, the child's fear becomes a sort of metaphor for the family's fear—a fear of confronting deeper or different problems. The blame for the problem cannot be assigned to the child or any other one individual or couple of individuals in the family. The blame can be system- or family-wide.

What is important to keep in mind, however, is that just as the family's functioning is central to sustaining the problem fear, so it is also central to the elimination of the fear.

If you have a child who has a problem fear, it is not the intent of this book to make you berate yourself with cries of "What have I done?" or "It's all our fault!" The idea is to shift perspective *a bit,* so that the problems of the individual are seen in context and the causes are shown to be circular rather than a straight line of cause and effect. The intent of this book is not to admonish, but to encourage.

In short, if your child has a problem fear and you think that your family could be playing a role in sustaining the fear, then you should be heartened, for what the family does the family can undo. The means for dealing with your child's fear and whatever has kept it going may be within your grasp. The question that still nags, however, is who should be treated, the child or the family?

Treat the Child or the Family?

The Gollish family is at wit's end. The youngest child, Tyrone, suffers from asthma. Lately he's been suffering attacks more frequently and his parents have had to rush him to the hospital several times. It couldn't happen at a more awkward time. Tyrone's older sister Sheila has just gone off to college, and his father, James, is frustrated at work, having been passed over for a promotion.

It's not hard to see that there's some stress in the Gollish family, and that it's finding an outlet in Tyrone's repeated hospitalizations for asthma, a disease that can be triggered by emotional factors. But what does the Gollish family do? Do they concentrate their effort on treating the asthma symptoms, increasing Tyrone's bronchodilating medicine and teaching him breathing control exercises? Or do they come to grips with what is really troubling the family, in the hope that Tyrone's symptoms will then ease?

Many families might just treat the symptoms, and they might be successful; but even if the symptoms disappear, they will not have dealt with what has been sustaining and exacerbating the symptoms. In the case of asthma, they do have to treat the symptoms—Tyrone is in acute physical distress and even danger—and they have to make sure there are no other physical elements, such as animal dander or cigarette smoke, triggering the attacks. *But* they should also deal with whatever emotional, family-system-sustained elements may be setting Tyrone off more frequently than usual. The family has to treat the individual *and* the context the individual is found in. First, Tyrone can take more individual responsibility for his symptoms (with a pediatrician's help) while the family loosens its need to "jump" on his asthma.

Some might agree that treating the individual and the family are necessary for asthma, but they think that in the case of childhood fears it is overkill—if you can get your child to go to the dentist without kicking and screaming, then what do you need to work on the family for?

The problem is, if a child's fear is being sustained by the family system's reaction to stress, then, though you may be able to eradicate that particular fear, you will not be treating a more sustained and troublesome issue. Unfortunately, that trouble won't go away, and it's likely to manifest itself again as another sustained fear (or psychosomatic illness, or behavior problem)—the family will simply find another way to enlist this child or another or another endeavor in its effort to maintain equilibrium.

In fact, childhood fears are not entirely analogous to asthma; unlike asthma, there is some question as to whether the fears need to be treated directly, on the level of the individual, at all.

Family systems theorists might argue that by dealing directly with the systemic problem manifested in the child's fear, you will remove the family's incentive for sustaining the fear, and the fear, deprived of its support, will go away. They might go even further, arguing that one of the problems is that so much attention is being focused on the child. Treating the child's fear directly, then, by such behavioral techniques as *systematic desensitization* and *modeling* might only maintain the focus and further sustain the family's problem.

It's our belief that the best way to deal with a child's problem fear, one that is disrupting the child's and the family's life, is to set the fear aside for the moment. The family should first try to figure out why the fear has been sustained, what role it is serving in the family, and how they can eliminate that role and take the focus off the child.

What Is Troubling the Family?

The actual "cause" of the fear is the child's temperamental tendency to be afraid, combined with either a traumatic experience or something he or she learned and a developmental matrix. The fear is kept alive, long after it should have vanished, by the family system's way of coping with a simmering conflict, and that conflict is usually either caused or stirred up by some stress affecting the family.

It's important to learn what stress is affecting the family so strongly. The most common source of stress is the family's life cycle and the rather awkward and demanding transitions that are required between each stage. These transitions mark the "comings and goings" of life. Also, each person within the family has his or her own developmental tasks to work on. The child is getting older, his or her parents are getting older, their parents are getting older, and each time they make the leap from one developmental stage to another there is stress in the family. And if a child's developmental demands coincide with changes in the parents' lives, as is often the case, then the stress will be much stronger and harder to cope with.

Within the family there are also the common baseline conflicts that every marriage goes through. These may be the result of some contretemps over the demands of work, or they may be about sex or money or—and this is a big one—the relationship between each spouse and his or her own parents and siblings. And there is the stress of parenting; this is especially stressful if the parents have conflicting attitudes about child rearing. Perhaps Mom is strict and Dad or Grandmother are lenient. This conflict, which may be rooted in other, deeper conflicts, will only confuse the child and divide loyalties.

Such stress is ongoing and expected. The source of stress precipitating a fear might not be so common and is more likely to be precise and acute rather than chronic and simmering. It may be that Dad has suddenly lost his job at the paper plant, or that a fire gutted the house and the family has to stay with relatives, or there may have been a death in the family.

To identify what is stressing your family, you often have to look closely at recent events, looking for all the more obvious stresses first—a new baby, a move to a new town, a new job, loss of a job, divorce, and any other comings or goings. The idea is to be aware of the family's life cycle and the changes and demands that it makes, and also to be aware that whatever happens to one member of the family has an effect on all the other members; though a stress may seem isolated to one family member it doesn't mean it isn't affecting everyone.

How does a family go about this? The best way to do it is through *communication.* People have to be honest and open, say how they feel and what they are experiencing, in order for the effects of stress to be known.

Determining what stress is at the heart of the problem is the first step. The next step is to examine the family's structure—the spatial coordinate—to see what in the family system would allow its response to a child's fear to be one that maintains the fear rather than dissipates it.

What Is the System's Role?

How a family copes with stress depends on the resources it can match against the demands that stress presents. Filling out the questionnaire included in Chapter 2 and looking at the functional and dysfunctional stress-coping strategies in Chapters 6 and 7 are ways for a family to identify problem areas. Do they have trouble communicating? Is independence encouraged in the family? Is power shared? Are roles flexible? All of these are characteristics of a family that is working well and they are resources that can be used against stress.

Perhaps the most important resource, as we saw throughout the chapters on stress, is an extensive social network and a strong support system. The social network can be measured in numbers—how many people is the family in contact with and what other groups are they a part of? The family's support system can only be measured in terms of quality—how supportive are friends, family, colleagues, and professionals?

Why are support systems so important? Because severe stress taxes a system's internal strengths very quickly. In fact, a stressful situation can present a family with problems it has never faced before; it may quickly use up resources that are needed just to maintain necessary functions, or it may require expertise and information that the family does not possess.

Using a support system is not a sign of weakness, but a sign of strength. The family cannot survive in isolation, especially in times of severe stress. Without energy, input, and aid from outside, the family can fall apart.

There are a few questions families should answer. Are they

"plugged into" a social network? Have they set up a support system? Are they using it? Can they ask, *Who can we get to help us?* Do they have access to friends, veterans, and experts?

There are many other family system traits that bear on the family's ability to cope with stress. How clear is the family's generational hierarchy? Who is in charge? Is there any blurring here? Do children have the power of parents? Do grandparents take over? Are parents as dependent as children? How are the boundaries between subsystems—are they too permeable (do parents or children invade each other), or are they too rigid (is the family divided into armed camps)? How about communications—are they open and free or closed off and restricted? And so important when it comes to childhood fears, are there cross-generational coalitions? An overly close parent and child? Are there triangles?

Identifying Triangles

No one triangle is more important than any other; just as one trait of a family system affects all other traits, so each triangle will reflect the structure of every other triangle to a degree. This means that if one triangle has soured and become unhealthy, this will be reflected in all the other triangles. Why? Because that is the only way the system can remain balanced.

Theoretically, if you are friends with Bob and Jane, and Bob suddenly stops being friends with Jane, then your relationship with Jane will also be affected—either you remain friends with her but stop being friends with Bob, or you remain friends with Bob and stop being friends with Jane. And it does not stop there. Your friendships with Sam and Carol, with Adrian and Max, also friends of Bob and Jane, will be affected. Thus, the split between Bob and Jane could split your whole group.

Of course, that's just in theory. The group will not necessarily split down the middle, since there are many other allegiances and bonds holding it together. If there weren't, every group would cleave on every contentious issue.

Nevertheless, this theory does apply to families to an extent—when one triangle becomes unhealthy, the others are likely to follow. Therefore, in searching for triangles in a family one can start almost anywhere; the problem affecting the family will affect every triangle.

In the case of a child with a problem fear, the first triangles to look at are ones the child is involved in, and of those the central one will be that which involves the child and the child's parents.

In the case of many system-sustained childhood fears, the child is often caught up in one of three types of unhealthy triangles. The child may be *triangulated*—caught in a war between two parents that is often ostensibly a battle over how to handle their child's fear (Mom is strict, Dad is lenient, or the other way around) when, in fact, it's just covering up their true conflict. Or the child may be caught in a *parent-child coalition* with one parent supporting the child and the fear to the exclusion of the other. Many times the child is the focus of a *detouring-supporting* triangle. The child's fear is used by the family system as a distraction from some unresolved conflict between the parents.

Again, this does not mean that the parents are to "blame." They did not "cause" their child's fear, nor did they "cause" it to persist and linger. The blame is systemic.

Treating the System

If your child has a fear that has become disruptive, and you think it might have something to do with how your family has reacted to it, there are five steps you should take.

1. Try to determine whether changes in the development of your family have challenged it. Are you in a transition phase between two stages (a child going to school, birth of a second child, grandparents moving to Arizona)? Are some members of your family at stages in their own development that might clash with the stages of others?

2. Look back at recent events and developments to see if there is anything that could have been particularly stressful, either for one member of the family or for the entire family together.

3. Take a close look at the structure of your family to see what characterizes it. Who is in charge? What are communications like? Are boundaries rigid or flexible, permeable or cohesive? Do parents act in concert? Do they have a life apart from the children?

4. Look at what therapists call *the presenting problem,* which in your family's case is a problematic childhood fear. The fear itself is not as important as your family's history of dealing with it. Specifically, what it comes down to is *how are you, the parents, dealing with the fear?*

5. Finally, ask the hard question and give it real attention. What would happen to the family or to individuals in it if the fear no longer existed? Who would fight?

Who would leave? Who would get depressed? Whose life would be empty?

We cannot emphasize enough that this does not imply blame. It is not that you are doing something "bad" to your child; rather, all of you are involved in a situation that, ultimately, is not the best for any or all of you. The good news is that the way you (child included) have been responding to the fear gives an indication of what you can do to take away the systemic support of the fear.

REWORKING THE TRIANGLES

We discussed the three types of triangles that can support fears: triangulated, parent-child coalition, and detour-supporting. (Detour-attacking, the fourth of Munchin's triangle types, is less likely to be important in a child's sustained fears.) We should look a little closer at what is wrong with them and how they can be restructured so that they no longer perpetuate the problem.

With triangulation, most commonly, one parent is strict and the other is solicitous; Mom tells Junior not to be a baby and to stop being afraid of the cat, whereas Dad gives in and says it's okay, he understands. Chances are that Mom and Dad have a deeper conflict than the matter of what to do about Junior's fear of cats.

The first thing Mom and Dad have to do is take Junior out of the corner of focus of the triangle. To do that they have to band together as parents and present a unified front to their child. Despite whatever disagreements they may have about parenting (or politics, style, attitude), they have to make decisions together regarding Junior.

When they do not make the decisions together, not only

do they pull Junior in opposite directions, which is confusing and disorienting for him, but they also, in a sense, give him equal status in the family, status inappropriate to his age. By making decisions together, they take their rightful places as the authority in the family, and Junior, probably quite relieved, is allowed to go back to being a child again.

With Junior out of the spotlight and his fear in proper perspective, Mom and Dad, using the good communications skills we outlined in Chapter 4, can address each other directly to find out what is really troubling them.

With a parent-child coalition triangle, Junior would have joined forces with one of his parents, perhaps Dad. Mom and Dad would no longer be at odds over how to handle Junior; Dad would have taken complete control and Mom walked away. Again, Junior's fear would be sustained as a way of keeping Mom and Dad from coming to emotional blows. Complicating matters, Junior probably would enjoy the attention and elevated status.

In this case, the solution might be for Mom and Dad to switch positions—make Mom take care of Junior and cater to his fear while Dad stays away. This is only an intermediate step, designed to unbalance the unhealthy triangle. The final goal would again be for Mom and Dad to stop being divided on the issue of Junior's fear. By coming together they would reduce Junior's status to an age-appropriate level, reestablishing the boundary between the generations.

Ironically, the trouble with the third type of triangle, detour-supporting, is not that Mom and Dad are divided over the issue of Junior's fear, but rather that they are so united because of it and are so focused on it that it has become a distraction from all other concerns. Their attention may even take the form of trying to help him with his fear. They may have worked out an elaborate behavior modification program to rid Junior of his phobia, which, of course, keeps the focus on him.

Again, the problem is that Junior has become the center of the family. He has the power, while Mom and Dad have become mere servants. If this is the case, the problem is not that Mom and Dad are not making decisions together—they are doing that—but that they have become obsessed with making decisions about Junior together, leaving them no time to make decisions about themselves.

To get out of this pattern, they have to realize that Junior's fear and its management has become an excuse for them not to communicate. Communication, and all the suggestions and guidelines outlined in Chapter 4, are again what is needed here.

Indeed, when it comes right down to it, good communication is what is always needed. With open and honest communication comes trust, and with trust comes the ability to listen to what the other person thinks and feels in a way that does not judge, and to talk to the other person about what you think and feel in a way that is not threatening. With good communications, conflicts do not stay submerged and unexpressed, only to appear down the road in a sustained childhood fear.

THE "HEALTHY" FAMILY

Good communications are central to the way a healthy family copes with their child's fear, for they cope in a way that does not allow it to become too much of a problem. Communications allow them to deal with all emotions and conflicts openly, and when a child is afraid of something, or beginning to feel in the least apprehensive, his or her parents know about it.

Whatever the fear is, no big deal is made about it. The

child's parents may use some simple behavioral techniques to calm down their little girl's fear of being sucked down the drain, or they may just let it pass on its own without too much intervention, for they know that most fears are developmental in nature and type and usually pass with time—*unless* too much attention is focused on them (which is why an elaborate behavioral regimen for reducing the fear is not always the best idea; it can heighten the already distorting focus on the child).

Whatever route the healthy parents take, they take it together. They do not let their child's fear and the question of how to handle it become a source of friction between them. Whatever their own personal beliefs (maybe Dad shares his daughter's fear of heights), they come together to present a unified position to their child.

WHAT IF THIS DOESN'T WORK?

If these suggestions do not work, the answer is not to abandon the principles. The temptation might be to say, "Well, this family business is all well and good, but I just want my child to stop fearing our golden retriever," and then to embark on an elaborate behavioral deconditioning program.

The reason these suggestions might not work is because following them is not easy. There is a compelling need for the present structure. Survival seems involved. It's hard to see yourself at all objectively, to see your family as a system. It's also hard to avoid seeing things in terms of cause and effect, to avoid searching for the one cause of a problem, the one thing or person to blame.

Sometimes a family needs guidance, someone from the outside who can see what it is they are doing and how they are doing it. Sometimes, a family needs help.

Behavioral Techniques

The behavioral techniques for treating fears are based on the theory that if fears can be learned, they can also be "unlearned." The basic idea behind all the various behavioral techniques is to make the child gradually feel more comfortable with the feared thing or situation.

Systematic desensitization involves teaching the child a series of relaxation exercises, which he or she can then use when encountering the feared thing or situation. The child is not thrown into contact in a sink-or-swim manner, but is exposed to an *anxiety hierarchy*—a series of steps, either real or imagined, ranging from mild to severe.

For example, a little girl who fears going to the doctor first imagines what it would be like if her mother told her that at some point in the future she will be going to the doctor. That would produce mild anxiety. More severe anxiety would be produced by imagining actually entering the doctor's office, playing with toys in the waiting room, and then being examined. As each of these steps is encountered, the child uses relaxation techniques to calm herself down. Slowly but surely, she progresses through the hierarchy, to the point at which the thing she fears no longer frightens her. The strength she gets from conquering the fear in her imagination should hold over into contact with the real thing.

Modeling involves having the child watch, in person or on film or videotape, someone else encounter the feared thing or situation. It is best if the person doing the modeling is a peer, and if that person is not a master of the feared thing or situation, but shares the child's initial apprehension. Best of all is when the child has a chance to join in when comfortable.

Self-efficacy theory is one way to explain why these techniques work. Both of them give a child a sense of mastery and control, a sense of self-efficacy. According to this theory, anything that gives children a sense of being able to handle things makes them less fearful. Of course, this is one of the primary goals of the family—engendering a sense of autonomy and self-esteem in the child.

Any of these behavioral techniques may be used by a family to deal with a child's fears. Indeed, most parents use similar techniques almost instinctively. If their boy is afraid of deep water they do not throw him into a pool, but let him scamper through a lawn sprinkler, then let him play in a wading pool, perhaps with a friend to make him feel better, then later take him into the shallow end of a pool or the first few feet of ocean water. They make sure that it all proceeds at the pace he sets and they do not press him to go any faster than he feels comfortable with. And above all, *they do not focus on it.*

There are a few things that should be considered before parents try out any elaborate behavioral techniques. It is vitally important that both parents work together and share the same convictions about what they are doing—one cannot systematically desensitize the child while the other reinforces the fear. Above all, they should be aware that *the treatment of a fear can easily become just as much of a distraction problem as the fear itself.*

These behavioral techniques, if used, should be used early on, before the fear becomes entrenched, before secondary gain arises, and before the family begins to use the fear for another purpose.

Some Suggestions for Specific Fears

STRANGER ANXIETY

Not all children go through this, although many do, usually between seven or eight months through to the end of the second year. It only becomes a problem if it's very severe—limiting the child's or the family's activities—or if it lasts much beyond the second year in a form stronger than simple shyness. *To prevent:* children should be regularly exposed to new people and situations from an early age. The fearful child should be gradually introduced to new people and situations, but by no means should be forced into contact. *Systemic considerations:* how does the family in general feel about strangers? Is there some family crisis that has encouraged all family members and not just the child to close up and put up protective barriers? Is the child a 'stand-in' for a shy parent?

SEPARATION ANXIETY

Common in the child's second and third years. *To prevent:* the child's security must be emphasized. The parents should provide a strong sense of trust and caring, and at the same time encourage autonomy and a sense of individuality. The intellectual concept of permanence can be reinforced with peek-a-boo and coming-and-going games. Above all, the child requires the assurance of support along with the encouragement of individuality. *Systemic considerations:* is the child afraid of separation because he or she has lost a sense of trust and protection? Does the child sense that the parents don't want him or her to separate from them? Does the child feel threatened by a new sibling? Is the child in a close coalition with one of the parents who is lonely because the other is remote?

SCHOOL PHOBIA (YOUNG CHILDREN)

When the child is young, this is usually a manifestation of separation anxiety. The source of the fear can be determined by taking the child through the day to see what it is really feared. Does Johnny show anxiety about getting up, but not so much about actually being at school? If so, then the separation is probably the problem. *To prevent:* basically the same as for separation anxiety, with the additional directive that the child must be encouraged to go back to school as soon as possible— the longer it takes, the worse it gets. Secondary gain for staying home must be removed—no TV, no getting out of homework, no special privileges, treatment, or attention. Going back to school can be done in stages; the child can sit in the principal's office for a while with a parent, then the classroom with a parent, and eventually the classroom alone. *Systemic considerations:* is the child involved in a too close coalition with the parent who will be alone in the house when he or she goes to school?

SCHOOL PHOBIA (OLDER CHILD)

If the child fears school itself, it is important to find out exactly what is frightening at school. For the older child, it is often some form of social performance anxiety—fear of tests, fear of failing, fear of being unpopular. *To prevent:* encourage the child's sense of self-esteem and competence. Also, check the child's study skills, abilities, and teachers; maybe the youngster is afraid of poor performance, or a teacher expects too much.

Again, slowly reintroduce the child to the feared situation, allowing him or her to set the pace. Professional help may be necessary. *Systemic considerations:* is there something stressful that the child's fear is distracting the family from coming to grips with?

FEAR OF MONSTERS

Common and normal among four- to six-year-olds. *To prevent:* it cannot be prevented entirely, but by monitoring what a child reads and sees it can be controlled to a degree. It is not a matter of censorship, but rather of postponing certain stories for when the child is older and will not think of monsters as so real. You can show children what is real and what is not without discounting their fears, keeping in mind that monsters for them are very real. *Systemic considerations:* is the fear being used as a distraction? Is there a recent stress the child is struggling to concretize?

NIGHTMARES

Deal with what in the nightmare is scaring the child, whether it is separation, monsters, or heights.

FEAR OF THE DARK

To prevent: allow the child to keep the door open and have a night light on in the hall, both of which are good safety practices. Demonstrate that there is nothing in the dark to be afraid of. Explain the sounds that the child might hear and emphasize the good aspects of the dark—it is peaceful and lets you get to sleep. Over a period of several nights, reduce the intensity of light in the child's room (from a 40 watt bulb, to a 25 watt, to a 10 watt, to a light out in the hall), at a pace that the child feels comfortable with. Do not encourage the child to join the parents in bed. *Systemic considerations:* is the fear being used as a distraction? Are the noises and talk in parents' bedroom both compelling and frightening?

FEAR OF DOCTORS AND DENTISTS

To prevent: don't add to a child's natural apprehension of being poked and prodded by saying it will not hurt, especially when, in the case of getting a filling, it can indeed hurt. Let the child express fear and gain mastery over the situation, by going slowly, using modeling (imagining a favorite hero going through the procedure may help), or simply bringing a favorite toy. *Systemic considerations:* is the fear being used as a distraction, as a way to draw parents in? Or is there recent family stress related to illness?

FEAR OF HEIGHTS

To prevent: make the child accustomed to encountering heights by climbing stairs or playground equipment or getting a view of things from father's shoulders. Use modeling and a gradual introduction to heights to give the child a sense of mastery over them. *Systemic considerations:* is the fear being used as a distraction?

FEAR OF ANIMALS AND INSECTS

To prevent: teach children that insects and most animals are smaller than they and are likely to be afraid of them. For those pets that are big, introduce the child to them early and teach proper techniques in handling the pet. Often the traumatic experience that a child has with a pet is a direct result of not knowing that pulling its tail would make it angry. Gradually introduce the child to the animal, again letting him or her set the pace. *Systemic considerations:* is the fear being used as a distraction or is there a recent experience with loss?

FEAR OF STORMS

To prevent: show enthusiasm for them and interest in them. Do your best to explain them at the child's level of understanding. It is hard to gradually desensitize a child's fear of storms, since weather cannot be produced on demand; but taking a child through an imaginary storm, from hearing a weather report to seeing lightning and hearing thunder, can help. *Systemic considerations:* is the fear being used as a distraction? Is thunder at night a substitute for nighttime parental bedroom noise or anger?

FEAR OF WATER

To prevent: introduce your child to water at an early age. Baby swimming programs, however, may not be the best idea. The automatic swim reaction disappears after a while, the child will not remember a bit of it, and it can be an unpleasant experience for the child. Gradually introduce the fearful child to more water, from a sprinkler to a wading pool, and eventually to the shallow end of a pool and beyond. *Systemic considerations:* is the fear being used as a distraction and a focus for parental collaboration?

9 When to Get Help? From Whom? For Whom?

There is an old saying: "If you wonder whether you should see a psychiatrist, you should go see one, then he or she can help you decide whether you need to come back." This carries a certain amount of wisdom when applied to the area of childhood fears. If you are not sure whether your child's fear warrants seeking a professional opinion, you might seek such an opinion to be sure. It won't hurt, and it certainly might help.

There are many instances in which families can benefit from professional help. A child's fear might be so overwhelming that it has distorted normal family operations. Perhaps little Shosha is so terrified of vampire bats that she is unable to be in the dark, or go to sleep, or go outside. Or the fear may not be as intense, but it may have lasted so long that it threatens to become a permanent part of family life. Or the family under stress may simply feel overwhelmed by the demands of coping with the child's fear. Or the stress is so great that all family members are afraid. Or the parents are too conflicted to agree what to do. Or, of course, the child may simply find the anguish of fear intolerable. Or the fear may be only one of a number of areas where the child is suffering or having difficulty.

People tend to think they should be able to handle such matters themselves and, as noted in the previous chapter, in most instances families can provide all the help that's needed. This is most likely the case with the family that is working well and that has adequate coping skills. *But* remember, one of the most important characteristics of a family that is working well is its ability to tap into its social network and make use of support systems, its willingness to go outside for expert help when needed. In other words, a key sign of a family's health is its willingness to get professional help.

Unfortunately, when it comes to psychological and emotional problems, most families, even basically healthy ones, are not so willing. A family with elaborate, strong social networks and support systems usually does not hesitate to turn to Uncle Harry the accountant to sort out their tax problems or, through a string of recommendations, search out a good orthopedic surgeon to treat a young daughter's scoliosis. There is, however, still a tendency to draw the line when it comes to problems that have even the smallest hint of a psychological nature. According to the Yankelovich American Family Report—the summary of extensive public opinion surveys in the late 1970s—most American families are still very reluctant to seek professional help for psychological problems and do so only as a last resort.

Sadly, mental and emotional problems still carry a stigma, even though psychiatry is now a well-established medical specialty that has proven invaluable in treating countless disorders.

Why do emotional disorders still carry a stigma? To find the answer we could search back to Plato and Aristotle and the pre-Socratic philosphers before them. Basically, it comes down to a dualistic view of humankind: we look at problems of the mind in one way and problems of the body in another. It is the "mind" that defines each person—the "me," the "I"—and we feel we have responsibility for it. Whereas our bodies are beyond our control.

Unfortunately, this leads to the concept of "blame" and

"fault." If a person comes down with a cold, he or she is not to blame. But if the person should, say, develop a pathological fear of water, that is something the individual should have been able to deal with. It is a sign of weakness. It *is* the person's fault.

Happily, this view is slowly changing. We now know that rather than being two separate entities, mind and body are really unified, more of a single mind-body. We know that bodily health affects emotional and mental health, and vice versa. Any number of physical disorders, ranging from nutritional deficiencies to hormonal imbalances, can cause serious mental disorders. By the same token, doctors and hospital workers have long known that patients' mental state plays a major role in their physical recovery.

Still, the stigma related to psychological problems has not been erased completely. Consider the case of schizophrenia, a disabling psychiatric disorder that affects approximately one out of every one hundred Americans, some 2.5 million people in all. Only recently has schizophrenia been brought out of the closet; only recently have families begun to admit, without shame or embarrassment, that they have a schizophrenic family member. The media have given considerable attention recently to the fact that schizophrenia is primarily a metabolic disorder, meaning it is a physical, and therefore socially acceptable, disease. And the media have only done this because families with schizophrenic members have found strength in banding together into forceful local and national advocacy groups that have heightened awareness of what is known of the disorder.

There is some hope that eventually *all* psychological disorders will be destigmatized. Ideally, families should be just as willing to seek a professional opinion about psychological distress as they would to search out information and guidance on hearing impairment, diabetes, or any other clinical disease.

What Kind of Professional Help?

PHARMACOLOGICAL

Ironically, a drawback to destigmatizing psychological problems by viewing them simply as upsets in body chemistry is that "chemical" solutions are sometimes considered *the* answer. Medication has accomplished an incredible amount over the past few decades. Schizophrenia, in many cases, can be partially managed with a drug regimen. Antidepressants have eased pain in countless lives. Looking to the future, some would say that as every human thought and emotion can be reduced to a combination of chemical and electrical transactions in the brain, the ultimate way to cure a psychological problem, such as a fear or phobia, will be to take a medication that removes that particular chemical and electrical equation from the brain.

Unfortunately, medications currently lack such surgical precision. They may be able to overcome psychological symptoms, but in the process, other organs or functions also may be affected. In a sense, medication is like blunt instruments that work by bludgeoning—somewhat akin to lopping off an arm to take care of an arthritic wrist, or shooting a mouse with an elephant gun. In most instances although drug therapy controls the symptoms of a disorder, the social, behavioral, and interpersonal problems are likely to continue. This does not imply that there aren't many instances in which medication should be used, but first there must be a clear determination that the potential benefit far outweighs any risks or adverse effects. It is also likely that psychological change and learning themselves change brain chemical reactions. Even with medication, a human interaction is critical for compliance and therapeutic interventions still deal with the problems of living.

THERAPY

Since the mind-body relationship works both ways, any psychological problem can, theoretically, be approached from either direction. We could, with the right medication, correct, for example, a problem of low esteem. Or through psychotherapy, a person could improve his or her sense of self-esteem, which, in the brain, might be manifested as a particular electrochemical reaction. There are medications that ease anxiety, panic attacks and some fears, but drugs that are highly specific without side effects are still a long way off. Thus, the various forms of psychotherapy are still crucial to the treatment of many classes of psychological problems. And even if we had more satisfactory drugs, it is unlikely that they alone would suffice. After all, we do not treat other more definable organic diseases with drugs alone. Insulin, for example, may be crucial in controlling diabetes, but it does not remove the need for physician-patient interactions.

Medication therapy and traditional psychotherapy focus on the individual; both are based on the patient-symptoms-disease model—a person carries the symptoms, therefore it is the person who's treated. What this ignores, and what we have been talking about throughout this book, is that individuals do not exist in a vacuum. A great measure of who they are, how they behave, think, and feel, depends on who is around them. This is an ecological model.

Psychological problems, if not *caused* by a distressed family situation, can at least be sustained by it. Treating just one member of the family system, however, can increase the tension in the family and exacerbate the situation. For one thing, the person in treatment might grow at a rate the others can't keep up with.

Imagine that Mom and Dad are having problems; Mom feels alienated, Dad lonely. Dad's going to a psychiatrist on his own to sort out his loneliness. This may only increase Mom's feeling of alienation and jealousy, for now Dad is sharing intimate secrets with someone else and is growing beyond the point where he was stuck, and Mom is not. But if they go together, they may be able to modify what is going on between them that is making them both feel unconnected. To expand on this: perhaps son Tommy refuses to go to school because he is in a too close coalition with Dad, which has developed because of his sense of loneliness. Taking Tommy into therapy to coax or coerce him into going back to school may only increase the tightening bond between father and son, and thus Mom's sense of ostracism. At the same time, it makes Dad more desperate than ever while Tommy is in school, and Tommy becomes increasingly unable to concentrate because he is so worried about Dad.

Does this mean that individual therapy is useless? Far from it. It is still the orientation most often recommended. It can be very important, but we feel it should not get in the way of the family's work, nor add to their problems. One alternative that has worked is therapy that concentrates on the context first, namely, *family therapy.*

The basic goal of family therapy is to enable family members to live with each other in a manner more adaptive than the one at present. Traditional psychotherapy maintains that only by understanding, accepting, or changing oneself can one learn how to live with others. There is some truth to that, but treating just one person does not treat the system; indeed, it can worsen problems within the system. Augustus Napier and Carl Whitaker, two prominent family therapy theorists, wrote in *The*

Family Crucible what they considered to be the ideal way to conduct therapy:

> Ideally, we would like to start with the largest system we are able to assemble. For example, if we discover there is a war going on between the two families of origin, it is preferable to start therapy at that level. After the two branches of the family are no longer at war, we concentrate on the nuclear family that initially got in touch with us. When the children have been disentangled from the couple's problems, we may work for some time with the couple. When there seem to be *no* further pressing relationship battles and when our allegiance to the entire group is well established, we can then work with individuals. But individual therapy should be like the Ph.D.—the last stage in training. Individual therapy is for the person who has learned to live with others and now wants to work further on living more comfortably with himself.

Another important reason to turn to family therapy is that it removes blame, but not responsibility, from individual family members. A person in therapy alone can fall prey to the temptations of finger pointing, either at himself or herself or others, without being able to see that blame is counterproductive because no one person is to blame—everyone is intertwined. Some therapists fall into the trap of accepting one family member's experience of another's reality and collude in blaming when what they have is really a subjective description needing further exploration.

This may make it seem as if there is a war of sorts between traditional psychotherapy and family therapy, and indeed, for a time, there was. Among some camps, considerable disagreement remains. However, more and more, the two areas are coming together. By one estimate, family therapists spend up to 50 percent of their time engaged in working with individuals. On the other side, individual therapists are, more and more, bringing spouses, children, and other relatives into their treatment of individuals to see what light they can shed on a situation. In the future, there will be an even greater synthesis of the two approaches.

At present, however, though these two approaches in the mental health field may be coming together, other fields are still keeping them apart—insurance companies require individual patient diagnosis for reimbursement, the legal system considers only "the best interests of the child" and not the family. They are stuck in the rigid individual model of therapy.

Many families who could derive tremendous help from family therapy are reluctant to enter into it. Fathers are particularly difficult to enlist. This is a problem shared by all forms of therapy, but family therapy faces an additional barrier: many people simply do not know what it is. Certainly family therapy has not received the media coverage enjoyed by other forms of therapy. Many people mistakenly think of it simply as a setting—therapy with the whole family sitting in—rather than as an altogether different way of approaching a problem.

What Is Family Therapy?

As its name implies, family therapy is a way of treating the whole family, a way of looking at problems of the individual as manifestations of the problems of the whole. There are several different schools of family therapy, but all share the same goal and the underlying belief that, as Nathan Ackerman wrote in

1958, "The family is the basic unit of growth and experience, fulfillment or failure. It is also the basic unit of illness and health."

Family therapy began shortly after World War II, a time when psychiatry, which had long been looked at with skepticism, was becoming a widely accepted and established ideology. As noted family therapy theorist Philip Guerin writes, "As soon as any ideology becomes established, professional outsiders—'change merchants'—in the field become impatient with the limitations and set out to establish new frontiers and new ways of thinking."

What frustrated the change merchants in psychiatry were the discipline's failure in treating schizophrenic families and delinquent children; they began to look for new ways to treat them. Ackerman, considered the "father of family therapy" for his work in the thirties and forties on the family and the interrelatedness of people, pointed toward a new approach—looking at the individual in context instead of all alone. In the 1950s, Ackerman and others embarked on what was known as the "family movement." It was a "movement" because change is always resisted, and like all movements, in the beginning it was underground. Murray Bowen, a family therapy pioneer, wrote:

> A psychoanalytic principle may have accounted for the family movement remaining underground for some years. There were rules to safeguard the personal privacy of the patient/therapist relationship and to prevent the contamination of the transference by contact with the patient's relatives. Some hospitals had a therapist to deal with the carefully protected intrapsychic process [the close one-to-one relationship between therapist and patient, attempting to determine the root of the patient's problem], another psychiatrist to handle

the reality matters and administrative procedures, and a social worker to talk to relatives.

To work under these rules, all family therapy was initially done solely under the aegis of research; it defied too many traditions, challenged too many deeply felt beliefs to be studied and applied directly and openly. Nevertheless, the movement began to grow, albeit slowly. By the late 1950s, there were family therapy groups in California, Topeka, Washington, D.C., Baltimore, Philadelphia, Atlanta, and New York.

TYPES OF FAMILY THERAPY

Today there are several relatively distinct schools of family therapy. Ackerman's type is now commonly known as the *psychoanalytic school* of family therapy, so called because it strives to have the family achieve its own insight into how it has evolved.

Although this school contributed a great deal, it had trouble developing basic principles and a training method. Nathan Ackerman died in 1969, and over the years his followers have not maintained his strong allegiance to psychoanalytic principles. Their style is now more akin to that of the *communications school*, which was, in fact, begun partially as a reaction to the psychoanalytic nature of Ackerman's work.

Founded on the West Coast by such pioneers as Don Jackson, Gregory Bateson, Virginia Satir, and Jay Haley, the communications school was primarily systems oriented. This school was not as concerned with insight into what had happened in the family's past as with what was going on at present in the family system. Their emphasis was on working with the family to open up lines of communication and how to keep that communication nonaccusatory (the language of acceptance).

The *structural school* was founded by Salvador Minuchin, late of the Philadelphia Child Guidance Clinic. Rather than concentrating on what the family members say to each other, or even how they say it, Minuchin and his followers concentrate on the patterns of communication, which in turn lead to structural patterns in the family, primarily the various triangles. Minuchin and his followers consider the family an organization and look at coalitions, boundaries, and hierarchies in the system as well as the additional spatial dimensions of closeness and distance. The technique of the structural school is to break the habits and patterns, to encourage new structures to take shape and come into use, and therefore to allow for healthier, more flexible individual and family development. In some ways, the focus is not on the messages but on the switchboard.

Murray Bowen founded the *differentiation* or *family systems* school in Topeka, then moved it to Washington, D.C. Unlike the other schools, which are ahistorical (it doesn't matter what happened in the past), Bowen *is* concerned with family history, his theory being that certain patterns get passed on from generation to generation. For people with experience in individual therapy, or who think of therapy as "talking," the differentiation school style may be surprising. Instead of having people "talk" about their past, the family is present as a living example of its past. The goal of this school, as its name suggests, is to *differentiate* the generations and the individuals within a generation, so that each succeeding generation in a family does not have to follow in the previous generations' footsteps.

Other, smaller schools are found throughout the United States and Europe, often centering around one therapist. Carl Whitaker, when he was at the Atlanta Psychiatric Clinic, began what could be called the *experiential* approach, based on Whitaker's belief that for a family to make progress it must have an emotionally meaningful experience in therapy. To this end, Whitaker recommends that the therapist become deeply involved in the therapy, essentially joining the family as a new parent. His approach is intuitive and, therefore, highly individualized and not easy to teach.

In this book, we have drawn upon almost every family therapy approach—from the importance the Ackerman school puts on the family understanding itself, through the communications school's emphasis on open, honest, nonaccusatory communication and Bowen's idea of separating the generations, to Minuchin's concentration on structure and restructuring.

This type of amalgamation is fairly common; many family therapists today do not subscribe to a single school, but pick and choose from all of them, finding a combination of approaches that works best for them and the families they work with. Principles include the fact that the "action" is between and among people and that there are inevitable patterns established, with regard to organization or communication or sequences of behavior.

THE TECHNIQUES OF FAMILY THERAPY

Family therapy techniques vary according to the family, the therapist, and the type of family therapy he or she practices. Currently family therapy techniques are often lumped into two groups—structural and strategic. Structural family therapy follows the ideas of Minuchin; strategic basically includes everyone else.

Structural therapists are not particularly interested in the specific symptoms or problem presented to them, nor do they care what happens outside the session. What they try to do is create *enactments* within the session that demonstrate how the structure is off track. The family is facilitated to "do what it does" right there in the session. The therapists take a very active, "hands on" approach, trying to introduce new patterns and effect change in the family system during the session and not necessarily with the family understanding or having an idea of what caused it to happen. The family drama is performed and rewritten.

The strategic therapist focuses on the symptoms and the family system's way of maintaining them. They give home-work—tasks that are to be worked on outside of the sessions. To them, the session is a kind of classroom where instruction is given, whereas life at home is where the lessons are really learned. Sometimes the instructions given may seem difficult or confounding, but they are designed to provoke quantum changes in the family rather than small, incremental steps.

A TYPICAL FIRST SESSION

Whether the therapist has a strategic or structural bent, there are often four stages to an initial interview—social, problem, interaction, and goal setting.

The *social stage* of the first session is the first several minutes, in which the therapist, as congenial host, greets the family members and tries to make them all feel at ease. This means talking to each individual family member in turn, usually beginning with the parents (or whoever can be immediately discerned as "gatekeeper," or most appropriate boss), giving each person attention, and speaking to each in an age-appropri-ate way. At this time, the therapist sets the ground rules for how the members are to conduct themselves.

It is also the time for the therapist to observe the family before the session really begins, and before the family members start behaving defensively or in the way they think they are supposed to in such a situation. The therapist may observe where each person sits. Is the symptom-bearing member isolated? Is he or she seated between the parents? Closer to one than another? Are the adolescents seated on the end, as if ready to make a quick exit?

In the *problem stage*, the therapist asks the family to describe the problem. He or she will usually go to each person in turn, often waiting to ask the symptom bearer last, both to give the symptom bearer time to formulate a response, and to take the pressure off this individual. Now is the time the therapist begins to form an idea of what the problem is. He or she will be looking for patterns—of communication, interruptions, agreements and disagreements; of attention and dismissal. This is when coalitions and triangles begin to become apparent. Do parents disagree, interrupt each other, compete for a child? If the family is concerned about a childhood fear, this is when a therapist might start to hypothesize what role that fear is playing in the family.

Throughout both the social and problem stages, the therapist is acting on a fairly apparent agenda; he or she wants to create a *therapeutic system* with the family. It's not easy. The family is a strong unit with powerful bonds and is very hard to break into, something the therapist must do if therapy is to succeed. The task can be likened to the demands made on an anthropologist who has to join a culture to find out how it really works and at the same time stay detached from it in order to observe it objectively.

For the therapist attempting to forge a therapeutic system, this means initially not challenging the family's beliefs and system; he or she adapts to it, plays along with its rules, becomes accepted, while at the same time observing what is going on.

During the *interaction stage* there is a distinct shift. In the two previous stages, the therapist was at the center of the conversation, whereas in the interaction stage, he or she may withdraw to become an observer, letting the family work on its own, watching them, searching for clues, patterns, and the like. The therapist may encourage *enactments* of how the family normally behaves. This stage can take time to progress. Family members will, at first, be reluctant to "let go" and behave as they normally do when at home by themselves. But once they get going, they are likely to take off.

At this point, the structural and strategic therapists take separate paths. Once the key pattern has been identified, the strategic therapist may go on to the final stage of goal setting, whereas the structuralist will try to direct a change in the structure then and there. There are three common "restructuring" techniques—boundary making, unbalancing, and complementarity.

With boundary making, the structural therapist may try to bring down the barriers between some people while putting up barriers between unhealthy relationships. Unbalancing involves the therapist "shaking up" the power structure, such as siding with a weak family member to give that person more power. Complementarity involves challenging the family members' sense of themselves as rugged individuals, demonstrating their interconnectedness.

In the final, *goal-setting stage,* both structural and strategic therapists sum up what they have learned in the session. The structural therapist might tell the family to either practice the new structures they have worked up in the session, or not to do a thing until the next session. The strategic therapist will assign homework to be done for the next session, but will present the work in a way that does not as yet challenge the family's system of beliefs.

One technique used both by structuralists and strategists is known as *paradox*. It is particularly useful with families that are defiant and very reluctant to change. Instead of telling a family how it should change, the therapist often prescribes the symptoms, directing the family members to do exactly what they are already doing. In effect, the therapist will agree with the way the family has chosen to function and will encourage it to continue because, in fact, within the family's system *it makes sense*. There is a very real investment in the status quo.

If, using a very simplified schematic example, a young girl has a pathological fear that is being used by the family to distract it from a conflict between the parents, the therapist will not say it's unhealthy; (why do you need a therapist to say *that?*) instead, he or she will first give it a *positive connotation*, saying it's admirable, complementing the child for sacrificing herself for her parents, and congratulating the parents on successfully handling a situation that would otherwise tear the family apart. In fact, the therapist will tell them that their "problem" is so good, that they must make sure they do not change or they will risk certain catastrophe. (This is likely the very thing they fear.) The defiant family is caught in a bind. Such families bristle at being told what to do and so do the opposite. Told to stay unhealthy, they defy the order and become healthy.

In sessions after the first one, the social and problem stages of the interview may be shortened—the therapist will know who the family members are and also have an idea of the nature of the problem. But these stages are still important; the social stage is a good time to observe the family at ease, and the family's perceptions of the problem may change. Nevertheless, the focus of the subsequent sessions will be the interaction and goal-setting stages.

The experience of being in family therapy may vary from therapist to therapist, and family to family. Some therapist may try to understand (a more conventional and expected approach); others may give confusing instructions or homework. Some may help you enact your drama during a session, while others may seem kind or remote, severe or detached. The problem may be dealt with head on, indirectly or may seem to be totally ignored.

Common Questions about Family Therapy

WHEN, WHERE, AND FOR HOW LONG?

Family therapy sessions usually take place once a week or once every two weeks, for an hour or more, in the therapist's office. Occasionally therapists will go into the family's home, where the family may feel at ease and not so reticent to talk. Therapists do not, however, like the potential distractions in the family's home. There is also the danger of complacency—therapy is work for the family and should not be treated lackadaisically. Also, as novice therapists soon find out, the family, as a unit, has incredible power and strength, but the therapist is just one person (although other therapists may be called in to consult on occasion), and so he or she may want to balance the strength by having the sessions take place on his or her turf. The therapist, given the difficult task of being asked to change painful life situations, must remain in charge even if it may not seem at times like the usual kind of leadership.

As for how long it will take, family therapy is oriented more toward a specific goal and task than other forms of therapy. The idea is not for the family to spend the rest of its years meeting once a week in a therapist's office. Therapy is usually embarked upon with some idea of when it will end.

On many occasions, all a family needs is a single session; perhaps all the family needed was a forum in which members could all air their views, thus giving them the confidence to begin communicating on their own, or there was a simple "rearrangement" that could be made in the organizational structure. Most families, however, come in for several sessions, usually over a period of a few months, and occasionally—but rarely—for a couple of years.

A therapist is concerned, however, that the therapy not end too soon. If the family has a serious problem (e.g., a father's depression, a ruptured marriage, a child's delinquency), the therapy may be long, hard work with results that are not quickly apparent. The fear is that the family might leave out of frustration, with the job only half done. Generally, when a family has accomplished what it needs to, the sessions will begin to wind down of their own accord. The family may also resolve an issue, feel better, leave, and return when they encounter another obstacle—much like going to your family doctor.

WHO'S INVOLVED?

Another commonly asked question is "Does the whole family have to be involved?" The answer, from most family therapists, is a resounding *yes* (at least initially). This is most certainly the case when the symptom is a childhood fear; but if any problem involves one of the children, obviously that child needs to be involved in the therapy. This extends to all people who are directly involved in the problem. If it involves the grandparents, then they should come in. If it involves an ex-husband or ex-wife, then they too should be brought in.

It is a common mistake, however, to think that when the children do not seem to be directly involved—when the family's problem centers around the marriage, as is often the case—the children need not be included and the only people who need to see the therapist are the couple. Or if one child is symptomatic and another is "perfect," it will not seem necessary to bring the perfect child in to the session for fear the child may lose ground in school by becoming upset. But it is not so much a question of who needs to see the therapist, but *who the therapist needs to see.*

Even if the problem seems centered on the marriage it's highly likely that the children have been drawn into it and the therapist needs to see this and to hear their experiences and observations and see them perform in the family scenario. In the case of the "perfect" child, the family session is not complete without the perfect child to demonstrate what family system need he or she fulfills in this arrangement, and therefore what role the less-than-perfect child plays.

Not only are children part of the family and therefore an integral part of how the family functions, but they can also act almost as co-therapists. Often it is a child who will cut through all the words to the heart of the matter. As we get older and are socialized, we learn to hide our emotions and deny those of others—to be more politic. But children are very attuned to emotions—the tone of their parents' voices tells them volumes—and they can point to what is really going on, often surprising parents who thought they were hiding their troubles.

Without doubt, children, especially young, barely verbal children, can be challenging in sessions. Both parents and the therapist may find them disruptive. But if they are given room to play and things to play with, their presence can be very rewarding.

One of the major problems facing all families who consider trying family therapy is the reluctance of some members to go along with it. Sometimes it is purely a matter of scheduling and convenience, with family members widely scattered. In those cases, every attempt should be made to gather as many family members together as possible, if even for only a few sessions, or one very long one. The core group should always be all the members of one family who live together.

Family members may also be reluctant to join in simply because they are not comfortable with the idea of family therapy (often, when one member suggests therapy, another member *(usually father)* will reject it outright, which, of course, exposes an overt or covert conflict within the family). Some family therapists are very reluctant to work with a family unless all members are present. Usually, when told how vitally important it is for the health of the other family members, reluctant members will give it a try. Sometimes it may take a call from the therapist, who, trained in active listening and the language of acceptance, may be able to argue the case in a more persuasive and convincing fashion than another family member.

Occasionally, no matter how hard the case is argued, one or more family members will refuse to participate (or will refuse to allow children to participate, feeling that they should not have to hear adult problems). In that case, although the situation is less than ideal, many therapists will nevertheless proceed. He or she may often ask the members present to role-play the missing member, or the therapist may play that person. This can also be done when key family members live far away or are deceased.

The bottom line is that the more people that participate in the family therapy sessions, at least at the beginning, the more resources the therapist has to draw on. And the more information he or she has, the better the results.

"I'VE HEARD ABOUT ONE-WAY MIRRORS AND VIDEOTAPE . . . "

Often a therapist will call in one or more colleagues to *consult*. Perhaps the therapist needs confirmation of a hypothesis or wants a second or even a third opinion. Most therapists, aware of the complexity of family interaction and the fact that many things can happen at once, like to have the eyes and ears of other therapists to make sure nothing is missed. Or the therapist may feel too involved in the family and want an outsider's view. These consulting therapists often sit outside the room and observe through a one-way mirror. Sometimes they may actually participate in the session. Or they may do both, coming and going throughout the session. This way of working is not unusual.

Videotape has been a boon to family therapy. Originally it was simply used by the therapists to review their sessions and as a way to get consultation without having to have other therapists present behind the mirror during the session. Then some therapists began to give the tapes to the families so that members could see how they looked. (This can be even more unnerving than hearing your own voice on a tape recorder—"Is that what I look like to everybody?") Many feel that this does little to change the process. Many family therapists also teach and may, with signed consent, request permission to show a tape to a selected group of professional colleagues and learners. (This would likely be done as an example of a success.)

Advances in video technology can now make family therapy a bit like televised sports, with instant replays, freeze frames, split screens (showing how one family member looks while another is talking) and corner inserts (putting the face of one person in the corner of the screen while the others converse).

HOW TO PICK A THERAPIST

Just as some baseball pitchers are superior to others, so some family therapists are better than their colleagues. Family therapy crosses professional lines. It is practiced by psychiatrists, psychologists, social workers, nurses, and paraprofessionals. First, you should look at the credentials of the therapists you are considering. This is important; do not feel shy or intimidated. You wouldn't be afraid to ask a roofer for his credentials, so don't be afraid to ask the same of a therapist. You will want to find out if he or she has studied at a university, worked at any of the noted clinics, or with any of the pioneers or their noted followers, or belongs to the American Family Therapy Association or the American Association of Marital and Family Therapists.

Experience is important. Family therapy is not an exact science by any means, and who a person studied with and how long they have practiced makes a difference. It's not that young family therapists are not good at what they do, but this is an area in which therapists learn by doing, and so the more they have done the more they have likely learned.

Perhaps the most important thing you can do to pick the right therapist is to spend some time with him or her. Have a trial session; you are looking for someone you can get along with, someone who makes you feel like change is possible. Most of all, you are looking for someone who cares and gives you the feeling that the focus is your family's well-being, even though the caring may not be a nurturing kind, it might be a desire to get on with things in a sensitive way. It would be hard to imagine why someone would become a family therapist unless he or she cared about other people; nevertheless, you may sense that one therapist cares a bit more about you and your family than another one does.

HOW MUCH DOES IT COST?

Cost is obviously an important consideration. Unfortunately, family therapy is neither free nor universally available. It costs about the same as individual therapy, if not more (family therapists charge by the session, not by the number of people who come to the session). It should be noted that though some health insurance plans cover family therapy, others do not (or only do if one of the family members is hospitalized), unless a modification is made, designating one person as the "patient."

Many community health clinics have very skilled family therapists. It is also possible to work with a young novice family therapist who uses a more seasoned veteran as an occasional consult (much in the same way residents treat patients under supervision in teaching hospitals). Many cities have freestanding family therapy institutes, usually worth serious inquiries.

DOES IT WORK?

In a sense, this is what it all comes down to: does family therapy work? The answer empirically is yes, although no therapist would claim to have a 100 percent success rate. Sometimes the therapy just does not achieve the desired results. But for the majority of cases, family therapists do report success. Unfortunately, there has been little clinical study of family therapy comparing its success rate with that of other forms of therapy. This issue remains extraordinarily difficult to study.

Nevertheless, there are statistics to document the success of family therapy. In treating anorexia nervosa, Minuchin and his colleagues reported a 94 percent success rate in treating sixty cases of this disorder. The remaining 6 percent eventually recovered with additional individual therapy. Compare this with the high fatality rate of up to 20 percent in severe cases that go untreated.

Although statistics are not as yet available regarding the use of family therapy to treat childhood fears, the record of case histories is impressive.

Sally, age seven, had been doing fine at school and seemed to be enjoying it. But recently she has become frightened of going to school, and the fear has grown, to the point where she is now afraid to be out of her mother's sight for even a moment. When the family therapist saw Sally and her parents she quickly recognized the problem—Sally and her mother had formed a very close bond, whereas father was almost peripheral. The therapist devised a course of action to deintensify the mother-daughter bond that would then force the parents to confront each other. The therapist instructed the mother to act afraid and have Sally take care of her. To them it seemed a little silly, but the therapist knew that in fact this is exactly what was happening in the family; the mother, alienated from her husband, was

> *terrified of being alone. Sally picked up on it and refused to go to school, and was, therefore, taking care of her mother. A couple of weeks of this did the trick. Sally was no longer afraid of school, her parents were drawn together and went into counseling to work on their problems.*

There are even a few previously published case histories showing how family therapy has been used to treat problem fears. In *Treating Young Children in Family Therapy,* Lee Combrinck-Graham examines the case of Michael, a young boy who had trouble getting to sleep unless he was in his parents' bed and even more trouble getting to school in the morning—he would develop stomach pains shortly after waking. Once at school, his performance was fine.

His problems were traced back to the birth of his baby brother, Kevin, and the inevitable sibling rivalry that ensued. It seems that Michael, in response to the arrival of his brother, became more involved with his parents, getting entangled and enmeshed. His sleep and school phobia problems derive from the fact that his parents, in some conflict, are pulling him in two different directions—father gets angry when Michael does not go to school, whereas mother soothes him. The therapist decided the answer was to get the parents to work on presenting a united front while at the same time disentangling Michael from them and from his brother, giving him a stronger individual identity. It worked. His sleep disorder vanished, as did his school phobia.

We may remember that Freud's classic childhood fear case history was "Little Hans." Jay Haley, from the West Coast communications school of family therapy, has his own "classic" childhood fear case history, which, appropriately, is known as

"A Modern Little Hans." Haley describes a six-year-old boy's fear of dogs. With what might be considered something of a behavioralist technique, the boy was directed to find a puppy that feared boys and to teach it not to be afraid. This is much like the behavioral technique of *participant modeling,* in which a child loses his or her symptoms by watching another child master the feared object or situation, but a very clever version of it, for not only did it take care of the boy's fear but also shifted the structure in the family. By making the boy take care of himself, Haley removed the child from the parents' focus—the boy could no longer be used either as a battleground or as a distraction; changing the ecology restored focus onto the parents.

Still, we should remember that family therapy doesn't "cure" children's fears. Instead, it seeks to remove the secondary gain the family derives from the fear and that perpetuates it long after it should have vanished on its own. Will it do this every time? With every family? In every situation? Actually, it probably will.

It's not impossible for a young child to have a serious fear that lasts and yet has little to do with the family system's support of it. But it is more likely that how the family responds to the fear will have an effect. It will either help it go away of its own accord or will keep it going.

ARE THERE RISKS?

There are few risks with family therapy, but there are major consequences. When a family is restructured to remove a child and his or her fear from the spotlight, the child, while happy to no longer be afraid, may nevertheless resent not having the family's attention anymore. There can be an interim phase of discomfort for the family before it grows accustomed to a new structure, which is why it is important for families to see therapy through to the end. Whether a risk or consequence, it is unrealistic for family therapists to believe that all families should remain together under any circumstances. A consequence of family therapy for some is that the parents may have been avoiding profound issues and barely holding together. In these cases, the change that gets facilitated is a separation, but most likely with less destructiveness.

SHOULD WE DO IT?

Because of its beginning as something of an "underground movement," family therapy is promoted rather zealously by its supporters. Although most families who enter therapy only do so when they have a problem, some of family therapy's most ardent supporters would suggest that every family enter therapy, regardless of whether there are problems, just to see how things are going. (Psychoanalysts used to advocate the same for all individuals.)

This is unlikely to happen, and one of the reasons lies in the term "family therapy," for "therapy" implies treating something that has gone wrong. Perhaps if it were called "family enhancement" or "family intervention" it would be more universally palatable, an endeavor that families could make use of, even when they seem perfectly fine.

Ultimately, there are numerous reasons why family therapy, in good hands, could be tried, whether one's family "needs" it or not. On the other hand, there are few good reasons not to.

What It All Comes Down To

Whether you give family therapy a try or elect self-help, the central thesis of this book calls for thinking about how you and your children function in terms of your family, your connectedness. Just as you are not alone, so your child is not alone. If your child has a severe, life-disrupting fear, chances are your family has some reason for perpetuating and possibly exaggerating it. Most fears disappear on their own, or they are sensitively coped with in some way that keeps them at a manageable level.

When a child's fear does become a disruptive problem, it is important to remember that no one is at fault; no blame should be assessed. Even if the problem can be traced to a submerged conflict between the parents, that does not mean that they're at fault. Everyone in the family plays a part in the way the family works. Concentrating on an individual's responsibility is to miss the bigger picture.

What is the best way to handle your child's fear? Encourage trust, autonomy, and the most open, honest, and nonjudgmental, nonaccusatory communications possible. Encourage a positive outlook, flexibility, and self-esteem. Encourage the realization and use of outside sources of support and assistance from relatives, professionals, old friends, and people as yet unknown. And most of all, in the process encourage and remove the obstacles to growing and loving.

Summing Up

The normal fears of a child's development are transient. If they last too long, or become seriously disruptive, then you have to be able to take a look at yourselves and be honest. All may not be well. Try asking the following questions:

1. Has there been a real, threatened, or even symbolic coming or going?
2. If stress is affecting the family, is it:
   a. developmental (a birth, a child goes off to school);
   b. external (job loss, a move); or
   c. catastrophic (death, disaster)?
3. Is there triangulation reflective of marital conflict?
4. Is the triangulation used to avoid arguing?
5. Is either spouse's family of origin closely involved with the family (is one spouse more connected with his or her own parents and siblings than with his or her spouse and children)?
6. Is communication open and honest with both spouse and children?
7. Is outside help available, and if so, is it used?
8. Who does each parent turn to when he or she needs to confide in someone? Does everyone have someone?
9. Who helps when a favor is needed?
10. Do the parents have a life of their own away from the children?
11. When was the last time the parents went out on a date?
12. What would happen in the family or to the family if the fear were no longer there?
13. Do each of the parents or parental figures differ on how to resolve the fear?
14. Does each person communicate, at various times, with *each* other person in the family?

Selected Resources

Bateson, Gregory. *Steps to an Ecology of Mind.* New York: Ballantine Books, 1972. For those who like rich theory and breakthrough thinking, this is the "parent of them all" for family therapists, a struggle for lay readers, but worth the effort.

Caine, Barbara S., and Benedek, Elissa P. *What Would You Do? A Child's Book about Divorce.* Indianapolis: Youth Publications/The Saturday Evening Post Company, 1976. A brief, nicely illustrated book for young children experiencing the divorce of their parents; emphasizes feelings.

Carter, Elizabeth A., and Mcgoldrick, Monica. *The Family Life Cycle: A Framework for Family Therapy.* New York: Gardner Press, 1980. A detailed book for mental health professionals emphasizing the life cycle of the family and what can go wrong as the family develops over time. Some excellent chapters with attention to variations from the middle-class family norm.

Fassler, Joan. *My Grandpa Died Today.* New York: Human Sciences Press. For ages four to eight. One of the classics, aimed at helping children learn about death, often for the first time; a help for the grieving parent.

Fraiberg, Selma H. *The Magic Years.* New York: Charles Scribner's Sons, 1959. This is *the* classic about a child's psychological and emotional development during the first three years; beautifully written and fascinating.

Gardner, Richard A. *The Boys and Girls Book about Divorce.* New York: Bantam Books, 1981. A classic, sensitive book addressed to children and their divorced parents, answering the typical questions children might raise.

Gottleib, Benjamin H. *Social Networks and Social Support*. Beverly Hills: Sage, 1981. A good collection of articles, expanding on these new entries into everyday jargon.

Guerin, Philip J., Jr., M.D. (ed) *Family Therapy*. New York: Gardner Press, 1976. A collection of articles on family therapy with a wide range of topics dealing with everything from the history of the field to projections for its future.

Gordon, Dr. Thomas. *P.E.T.: Parent Effectiveness Training*. New York: Plume, 1975. Provides good guidelines of communication, showing how you can correct and praise your children in a way that enhances, rather than undermines, their self-esteem.

Greist, John H., M.D., Jefferson, James W., M.D., Marks, Isaac M., M.D. *Anxiety and Its Treatment*. New York: Warner Books, 1986. A good look at the nature of fear and anxiety disorders.

Hoffman, Lynn. *Foundations of Family Therapy*. New York: Basic Books, 1981. One of the best guides to the basic principles of family therapy and where they came from; interesting and enjoyable, but occasionally difficult reading.

Kellerman, Dr. Jonathan. *Helping the Fearful Child*. New York: Warner Books, 1981. A good look at the various behavioral techniques that can used to reduce a child's fear and anxiety from an individual point of view.

Lewis, Jerry M., M.D. *How's Your Family?* New York: Brunner/ Mazel, 1979. An important look at the differences between families that are working well and families that are troubled.

Liddle, Howard A. (ed) *Clinical Implications of the Family Cycle*. Rockville, Md: Aspen Systems Corp., 1983. A good collection for the professional by many of the leading theorists.

McCubbin, Hamilton I., Ph.D., and Figley, Charles R., Ph.D., eds. *Stress and the Family* (2 vols.; 1: *Coping with Normative Transitions;* 2: *Coping with Catastrophe*). New York: Brunner/Mazel, 1983. As its title suggests, a fairly comprehensive examination of the effects of stress on the family.

Minuchin, Salvador, Bernice L. Rosman, and Lester Baker. *Psychosomatic Families: Anorexia Nervosa in Context.* Cambridge: Harvard University Press. One of five or six books for practitioners by one of the innovative giants in the field. All practitioners know his work.

Napier, Augustus Y., with Whitaker, Carl A. *The Family Crucible.* New York: Harper and Row, 1978. A look at one course of therapy with one family, from beginning to end. It's startling, funny, moving, even actually thrilling at times; reads like a novel.

Patteson, E. Mansell. "A Theoretical-Empirical Base for Social System Therapy." In E. F. Foulkes, R. M. Wintrob, J. Westermayer, A. R. Favezza (eds) *Current Perspectives in Cultural Psychiatry.* New York: Spectrum Publications, 1977, pp. 217–253. Excellent summary of clinical applications of support systems.

Sarafino, Edward P., Ph.D. *The Fears of Childhood.* New York: Human Sciences Press, 1986. Another look at how behavioral techniques can be used to reduce a child's fears, with suggestions on how to handle specific fears; individually based.

Van Ornum, William and Van Ornum, Mary Wicker. *Talking to Children About Nuclear War.* New York: Continuum, 1984. A good introduction in an area in which more and more is and should be written. Other worthwhile articles are available.

Walsh, Froma, ed. *Normal Family Processes.* New York: Guilford Press, 1982. A book for professionals, aimed at bringing together concepts of normality from a family perspective, with many noted contributors. Variations in family structure and cross-cultural perspectives are discussed, as well as family changes over time.

Wass, Hannelore, and Corr, Charles A., eds. *Helping Children Cope with Death: Guidelines and Resources.* As its title suggests, this book presents guidelines for how adults can help children cope with death; it has an extensive annotated bibliography of works of fiction and nonfiction that could help children of all ages better understand and deal with death.

Weiss, Robert S. *Going it Alone: The Family Life and Social Situation of the Single Parent.* New York: Basic Books, 1979. A sensitive orientation to the special issues of being a single parent; easy to read, with frequent references to individuals and their situations balanced by helpful, reality-based generalizations.

Index